Psalms
The Sunrise of Hope

Bob Saffrin

Copyright © 2012 by Robert D Saffrin All rights reserved.

Printed in the United States of America

Unless otherwise noted all scripture is taken from the Holy Bible, New International Version®, NIV®. Copyright © 1973, 1978, 1984, 2011 by Biblica, Inc.™ Used by permission of Zondervan. All rights reserved worldwide. www.zondervan.com.

The "NIV" and "New International Version" are trademarks registered in the United States Patent and Trademark Office by Biblica, Inc.™

As noted some scripture taken from The Holy Bible, New Living Translation copyright © 1996, 2004, 2007 by Tyndale House Foundation. Used by permission of Tyndale House Publishers Inc., Carol Stream, Illinois 60188. All rights reserved. New Living, NLT, and the New Living Translation logo are registered trademarks of Tyndale House Publishers.

As noted some scripture taken from the NEW AMERICAN STANDARD BIBLE®,
Copyright © 1960,1962,1963,1968,1971,1972,1973, 1975,1977,1995
by The Lockman Foundation. Used by permission."

Cover image used by license agreement Dreamstime LLC

Cover design: Joy Christiansen

Authors note: Psalm 3 has been previously published under the title *How to Sleep Like a Baby, a Meditation on Psalm 3*. Psalm 23 has previously been published under the title *Psalm 23, Help for Lost Lambs*. Both are updated here and included as bonus content.

Contact Bob Saffrin at: www.bobsaffrin.com

Other books by Bob Saffrin:

Moses, Steps to a Life of Faith

Elijah, Steps to a Life of Power

Psalm 23, Help for Lost Lambs

How to Sleep Like a Baby, a Meditation on Psalm 3

Contents

FOREWORD	7
ACKNOWLEDGMENTS	11
INTRODUCTION	13
PSALM 3	**19**
Hope for the Sleepless	19
PSALM 8	**35**
Hope for the Insignificant	35
PSALM 13	**55**
Hope for the Hopeless	55
PSALM 23	**73**
Hope for Lost Lambs	73
PSALM 40	**97**
Hope for the Shattered	97
PSALM 42-43	**113**
Hope for the Despondent	113
PSALM 84	**129**
Hope for the Homeless	129

PSALM 91 143
HOPE FOR THE VULNERABLE 143

PSALM 107 173
HOPE FOR THE UNLOVED 173

PSALM 139 195
HOPE FOR THE POOR IN SPIRIT 195

ABOUT THE AUTHOR 211

APPENDIX 213

Foreword

When Bob Saffrin asked me to write the Foreword for *Psalms, The Sunrise of Hope*, my initial thought was, what would I write? I long ago earned a gold medal for being a negative, hopeless, disgruntled individual. Praise be to God, though, he took away that medal of defeat and promised me a heavenly crown of hope that will never fade away or be broken by life's heartaches. The Good News is God will do that for you too.

I first met Bob when he joined the John 3:16 Marketing Network. I always read the blogs of authors when they join and his blog post that day was about Moses. His simple but evocative writing style drew me into a familiar Bible story that stirred me emotionally and revealed God's truth at a much deeper level.

Trusting God through trials, believing God's promises when all hope seems lost, feeling worthless and abandoned — traumas like these can leave us feeling shattered and afraid. Can we really have, as Bob describes, "indestructible hope, a hope that is never crushed?" What could I share with readers that would help them see God's grace in the midst of sorrow and speak to their hearts in *Psalms, The Sunrise of Hope?*

Once I began reading, memories gushed forth of God's faithfulness in former battles that had threatened to destroy all my hope. Over a cup of coffee at Panera Bread, tears of thankfulness covered my cheeks as I remembered from where God had brought me.

Hope for the Shattered, Psalm 40 — "He lifted me out of the slimy pit, out of the mud and mire; he set my feet on a rock." I remembered the day in 1985 when I contemplated ending it all with pills. God spoke to me and reminded me — I died for you on the cross.

Hope for the Sleepless, Psalm 3 — My husband walked out on me and the next year I cried myself to sleep every night while clutching my Bible — "I lie down and sleep;

I wake again, because the LORD sustains me."

Hope for the Hopeless, Psalm 13 — I couldn't conceive and being barren was like a dagger in my heart—a curse. Did God even care?

These sorrows and many more are part of the desert wastelands I wandered in for years before God's Word became real enough to change me — for good. God had to do a lot to "fix me" — and because we have a God who loves us so much, he wouldn't leave me where I was — and if you are a vagabond in the pit of despair of broken dreams, he won't leave you there either.

From time to time, I take a peek at my past, the wretch that I was, lost in a swamp, and remind myself of the good work God has done in me. Fairy tales and Hollywood stories abound about kings — but God's story about the King of Kings is not a fairy tale—it's real. God is our heavenly father and he has adopted you. God wants to redeem you from hopelessness into a hope-filled child of God — he is your kinsman-redeemer, making you his son or daughter.

Let your heart be moved and your mind renewed. The Great Physician wants to do a miraculous surgery on your spirit. God majors on the majors—the seemingly impossible, the outlandish hope, the last chance. Don't let the slough of despair keep you from knowing the fullness of God's joy. Read the Psalms as never before in *Psalms, The Sunrise of Hope,* and be blessed to tears as I was. You CAN find hope because God loves you TOO MUCH to leave you hopeless.

> Lorilyn Roberts
>
> Founder, John 3:16 Marketing Network
> Author of:
> *Seventh Dimension, the Door*
>
> *Children of Dreams*
>
> *The Donkey and the King*
>
> *How to Launch a Christian Best-Selling Book, The John 316 Marketing Network Manual*

Acknowledgments

I am grateful to Barb Saffrin for proofing and editing and to Joy Christiansen for both editing the text and designing the cover.

I also want to thank the beta readers who graciously agreed to read and help evaluate the finished manuscript. Beta readers are: Karen Thomas, Patricia Day, Leslie French, Judy Van Zyl, Kara Howell, Sally Ann Bruce, Wendy Jones, Alicia Bridenbaugh, Kendra Stamy, and Makyra Williamson.

Mostly I want to thank the Holy Spirit for inspiring the wonderful Psalms and for helping me understand how they directly apply to my life.

Introduction

I always carry a Swiss Army Knife when I'm backpacking in the Minnesota wilderness. It's so much more than a pocketknife; it's a multi-tool and is useful for those unexpected trail emergencies. Think of this book as your spiritual Swiss Army Knife. Keep it handy, read it, study it, be familiar with the contents, and then pull it out for those times when life is confusing and raw. When you're struggling with problems, grab this book, turn to the Psalm that fits your moment and find hope on God's lap.

Christian hope is not a longing or yearning for God to help; it is not waiting for the slim chance that things may get better. Genuine hope is the confidence that God is in your life and on your side, now and forever, and that nothing can separate you from his love.

True hope is resting in the unending love of your creator, expecting him to act on your behalf.

In this book we will examine ten Psalms that all have the common thread of helping us find hope in the midst of difficulty.

Psalms are Hebrew poems that were set to music and used by the Israelites for worship, prayer, and expressing their emotions. Studying them helps us connect with God and understand his ways as we read how King David and others learned to cry out to God in the midst of their struggles.

Joined with faith and love, hope is an essential and fundamental element of the Christian life. Faith and hope are so closely linked that they cannot be separated and we find it difficult to discern the difference. Still, there is a difference between them. Faith is belief in the promises of God. Hope is a soldier; it fights for us as we wait for the goodness of God to accomplish his will in and for us.

Hope is the confident expectation, the sure certainty that what God has promised, he will deliver.

Each chapter of this book examines one Psalm, one tool in our spiritual Swiss Army Knife. I pray that as you enter into the emotions and experience the truths of these Psalms, you will be filled with hope as I have.

*Guide me in your truth
and teach me,
for you are God, my Savior,
and my hope is in you
all day long.*

—Psalm 25:5

Psalm 3

Hope for the Sleepless

How are you sleeping these days? I remember in my younger years I could sleep anywhere. I could sleep in a tree. I could use a rock for a pillow. It didn't matter. I could lay down anywhere and fall asleep almost instantly; these days, not so much. I sleep less and less as I get older.

Most of us have had times where stress has kept us awake. Unless you live in a bubble, you've been there. It's that nagging worry or circumstance that you just can't see your way through, or that fear that might materialize. You lay in bed and think, you worry, and you just can't hit the stop button.

I imagine King David had many sleepless nights in the Judean wilderness when he was being chased by his son Absalom.

> A messenger came and told David, "The hearts of the men of Israel are with Absalom." Then David said to all his officials who were with him in Jerusalem, "Come! We must flee, or none of us will escape from Absalom. We must leave immediately, or he will move quickly to overtake us and bring ruin upon us and put the city to the sword."
>
> —2 Sam 15:13-14

Absalom was David's son. The son had been conspiring against his father, the king. He wanted to overthrow his father and take the crown and the throne for himself. Can you imagine how King David felt as he was forced to run, to flee from his own son?

How does a person respond to such stress? In that wilderness, David had time to sit and contemplate; he had sleepless nights to cry out to God. It is in that wilderness that Jehovah gave David several Psalms, including Psalm 3, to quiet and comfort his spirit.

Psalm 3

If you have a reference Bible or a Bible with margin notes, you will see a little note below the title of Psalm 3: "A Psalm of David When he fled from Absalom His Son." David has left the palace; he is running for his life. He is crouched below a rock outcropping for shelter from the scorching sun in that Judean wilderness, and he grieves for what has become of his family and his life. As he pours out his heart to God he takes quill to parchment and writes:

> O Lord, how many are my foes! How many rise up against me! Many are saying of me, "God will not deliver him." Selah

> But you are a shield around me, O Lord; you bestow glory on me and lift up my head. To the Lord I cry aloud, and he answers me from his holy hill. Selah

> I lie down and sleep; I wake again, because the Lord sustains me. I will not fear the tens of thousands drawn up against me on every side. Arise, O Lord! Deliver me, O my God! Strike all my enemies on the jaw; break the teeth of

> the wicked. From the Lord comes deliverance. May your blessing be on your people. Selah
>
> —Psalm 3

The secret to letting go of stress and sleeping like a baby is contained within the words of this Psalm.

Several years ago on a plane headed for the mission field in India, I tried out a new pair of headphones that I bought for the trip. Twenty hours of flight time gave me an opportunity to relax and listen to some soothing music. I had bought my first pair of noise-canceling headphones and was anxious to try them out. I put them on my head, turned them on and was immediately startled with the complete silence. The constant roar of the jet engines was instantly cancelled, the sound depravation so dramatic that I immediately took them off and then put them on again just to experience the spectacular change.

Noise-canceling headphones are great, but what if you had a stress-canceling device? What if you had a fear-canceling device? Imagine canceling all your anxiety and troubles. How cool would that be? If you had such a device, could you sleep? I believe the Holy Spirit gave King David this Psalm to help him sleep as he faced one of the most difficult times of his life. Could it be that it will also work for you and me?

We find David in Psalm 3 exiled from Jerusalem and on the run. At night he lays down, not on his bed of royal comfort and luxury, but on the rough rocks of the hillside — on a bed of anxiety. We find David as he begins to write, despondent and filled with dread.

> O Lord, how many are my foes! How many rise up against me!
>
> —Ps. 3:1

I love that the Psalms are brutally honest. There is no false religiousness or piety. No conjured happiness. The psalmist just pours out his heart; he tells it like it is. If he's mad at God he tells him. If he's despondent, he expresses that to his Lord. The psalmist is simply real with God and that is a tremendous lesson for us. The Lord wants us to be authentic and real. You might as well tell God how you feel, he knows anyway.

I love this Psalm. It tells us that it is possible, in the depths of life's darkest experience, to still have hope in God — maybe even to get a good night's sleep! I can sympathize with David. These are possibly the most stressful days of his life. He can hardly believe it and he can't get his emotions around the fact that his own son is gunning for him. How did David feel about his son? Read his words when Absalom died: "O my son Absalom! My son, my son Absalom! If only I had died instead of you — O Absalom, my son, my son!" (2 Sam 18:33).

Can you imagine now how David felt, knowing his beloved son is out there hunting for him, trying to kill him? What a dagger it must have been in David's heart to have his son turn on him. David describes his problems, trials, stresses and pressures. His friends aren't much help; they are discouraged too.

> Many are saying of me, "God will not deliver him."
>
> —Ps. 3:2

Have you ever asked the question, "Where is God?" Maybe you are asking it today. Is there hope for us in God? Is there any help in the circumstances of life when we feel that everything is caving in on us and we can't cope with stressful days?

That's our David, the greatest king of Israel, crushed by his circumstances and defeated by his emotions. And what does he do? He goes to God and he pours it all out to him. He pours all of his stress, fear, and trouble out to Jehovah.

You know, sometimes I feel like the whole world is against me. But then when I think about it, I realize that it is not true. The whole world isn't against me — there are several smaller countries that are still neutral. Hey, it's the ailment of our age. The stress of life's pressure is the hallmark of twenty-first century living. I read somewhere that 43% of adults suffer adverse health effects due to stress.

According to USA Today, a survey of 501 adults was conducted by the Research and Forecast Syndicate, and they isolated the responses into these results with regard to what causes stress in people's lives. Believe it or not, no surprise to you I would imagine, right up there at the top was work.

Thirty six percent of people said that work was the biggest cause of their stress. Thirty-two percent, coming in a close second was anxiety about money. Ten percent said that children caused them the most stress. Seven percent said it was their ill health. Five percent said it was their marriage. Another five percent said it was their parents that caused them stress. Only five percent said they had no stress.

A typical bookstore tells the story. There are hundreds of books to help you manage the pressure of life. And there are more than books; there are DVD's reproducing sounds of forests, oceans, birds and rainfall to help calm us. Some try yoga and eastern mysticism, not to mention stress balls, stress beads, and body rollers that you roll up-and-down your head and back to relieve stress. We can conclude from all of this that many people in our society, including Christians, are not exempt and find it hard to cope with anxiety. It's no wonder we can't sleep. None of us are immune to stress. Anxious and fretful days can lead to sleepless nights.

Put yourself in David's place. Night after sleepless night, he lays on the rock of that

Judean wilderness, thinking about all he has lost. At night he thinks about his circumstance. There is no tranquility of mind, no peace. He goes over and over it in his mind. The hours slip by. No sleep tonight.

David is in danger of losing his kingdom, his wealth, maybe even his life. The great King of Israel has gone into hiding, running away from his problems. He has plenty of worry to keep him sleepless. What do you do when you experience those times that keep you awake? Do you run away? David ran away to the wilderness and bedded down on the rocks. We have more things to run to for diversion. Maybe you escape to television, or food, or alcohol? We would like the diversion of sleep but sleep evades us because we can't get away from our own minds and our minds won't allow us to sleep. What do we do?

What did David do? He prayed:

> But you are a shield around me, O Lord; you bestow glory on me and lift up my head. To the Lord I cry aloud, and he answers me from his holy hill. Selah.
>
> —Ps. 3:3-4

Notice the word "Selah" after verse four. Like most of the Psalms, these words were meant to be sung, and that little "Selah" is an interlude. But the Psalms are more than songs, they are also meant to teach us; and so, this "Selah" is also a place for the reader to stop and contemplate what was just read.

David prays. Notice that he doesn't pray "O Lord, please get me out of this mess?" That prayer would be okay. God is our father; he loves it when we come to him in our distress and ask for help. "Which of you, if his son asks for bread, will give him a stone? Or if he asks for a fish, will give him a snake? If you, then, though you are evil, know how to give good gifts to your children, how much more will your Father in heaven give good gifts to those who ask him!" (Matt 7:9-12).

When you are in trouble it is good to go to your heavenly father and ask for his help. But let me share something that I have learned. When you ask God for help he always gives it, but it is in his timing, it is on his terms and it may not be the help you were expecting. God always gives us precisely that which we need but not always what we ask for. Sometimes it takes a while to discern what God is doing. Help doesn't always come tonight. So here is the question — how do I sleep tonight? Do I just grit my teeth and say, "Lord I trust you for your help." Then do I just say to myself — "Sleep...Sleep!" You know that doesn't work. That will never put you to sleep. But that's not what David did. Look at the verses again:

"But you are a shield around me, O Lord; you bestow glory on me and lift up my head. To the Lord I cry aloud, and he answers me from his holy hill." He doesn't ask God for help at all. David is in more trouble than he has ever been in his life, but in his sleepless, restless, and anxious night he doesn't pray and ask God for help. What does he do? Read the prayer once more. He turns his focus away from his problems and turns his attention to the Lord.

He focuses on who the Lord is: "You are a shield around me."

He focuses on what the Lord does: "You lift my head."

He focuses on how the Lord is there for him: "I cry out and you answer me."

David begins to meditate on who the Lord is, what the Lord does, and how the Lord has always been there for him. He is anxious, afraid, disheartened, and he can't sleep, but he starts to meditate on these things. What is the result?

> I lie down and sleep.
>
> —Ps. 3:5

And then:

> I wake again, because the Lord sustains me.
>
> —Ps. 3:5

Wow! He sleeps like a baby and he wakes up refreshed. Are his problems solved? No! His circumstances haven't changed. How does David feel in the morning?

> I will not fear the tens of thousands drawn up against me on every side
>
> —Ps. 3:6

His fear and anxiety are gone even though his circumstances have not changed. We tend to think that if only things would change, then we wouldn't feel so bad. But think about it, his circumstances haven't changed at all. This is still the biggest struggle of his life. He is still faced with the same grief knowing that his beloved son has turned the whole nation against him. Nothing has changed — but David has changed. His outlook and emotions have changed.

It's a new day. How does David face his new day?

> Deliver me, O my God! Strike all my enemies on the jaw; break the teeth of the wicked.
>
> —Ps. 3:7

Now he asks God to help him with his circumstances. He asks God to strike his enemies, "An upper cut to the jaw, Lord, break their teeth." Yikes! But what is David really saying? Think about it. Who really was David's enemy? Was it Absalom? No it couldn't be Absalom. When Absalom died David cried out, "I wish I had died instead of my son whom I loved." Could David's enemy be all the people who had abandoned him and followed Absalom? No, it wasn't the people who had abandoned David to follow Absalom. Look at the next verse:

> From the Lord comes deliverance. May your blessing be on your people.
>
> —Ps. 3:8

David was a wise old king. He knew that bitterness toward his son or toward his people would only keep him awake. God had given him his son and his people to love, not to hate. Who then are David's enemies? In all of our struggles Satan and his army are our true enemies. "In your anger do not sin. Do not let the sun go down while you are still angry, and do not give the devil a foothold" (Eph 4:26-27). Listen friend, being angry at your circumstances or at those who put you in this fix will just keep awake.

No matter what you are going through, David gives us a recipe for how to sleep like a baby. The devil is on notice. He's done keeping us up. In this Psalm, David gives us a formula for sleeping like a baby in spite of our problems. By meditating on God himself, and turning our focus to the same three questions that helped David, we will find the same sleep he found.

Psalms, The Sunrise of Hope

1. Who is God?

2. What does God do?

3. How is God there for you?

When you can't sleep, go to this Psalm to read and meditate. See if God won't give you sleep that will refresh and sustain you just like David, so that in the morning you face your problems with a new-found faith and confidence.

Life Lesson

Knowing How to Defuse the Stress that Keeps Us Awake at Night

Consider and discuss: If you had to name only one, what is the worry or stress that prevails above the others in your life? What do you currently do to manage that stress?

When David couldn't sleep he changed his focus from his problems to the Lord. He meditated on:

1. Who the Lord is: "You are a shield around me."

2. What the Lord does: "You lift my head."

3. How the Lord is there for him: "I cry out and you answer."

The exercise in the appendix is patterned after what David did when he couldn't sleep; try it, meditate on the verses there, and see if you too will sleep like a baby.

Psalm 8

Hope for the Insignificant

This Psalm brings to mind some of my most intimate times with the Lord. My family has a cabin on a lake in northern Minnesota and we spend many summer days there enjoying nature. One of the things I love to do at the cabin is the midnight boat ride. With family or friends, we usually spend our evenings at the campfire and just chat and enjoy each other's company until late. Then we head to the dock, board the pontoon boat, and motor across the lake at dead-slow speed. We play soft worship music on the stereo as we idle across the lake in silence, each person enjoying their own experience with Jesus. I prefer the clear moonless nights, with very little peripheral light to pollute the rich blackness. The stars shine in a Milky Way setting of brilliant gems. As I slowly pilot the boat, navigating the darkness by the small dots of light on shore, I go through a familiar range of emotions. I look up at God's infinite vastness. In my spirit, I feel my own smallness as I realize that I am but one tiny speck on a small planet revolving around an unremarkable star in a third-rate galaxy among billions of other galaxies. But as I focus on the incredible beauty and contemplate its creator, I begin to hear his voice calling me. His Spirit speaks to my spirit — "You are my son. I am your father; and all that you see is your inheritance." For me, the midnight boat ride is a time to feel my smallness, but I also sense greatness, knowing that the one who created the cosmos is my daddy.

Many people feel insignificant. They don't believe that their lives matter much. They think, "If I cease to exist how many would even notice." If this is you, then you are missing a very important truth. If you ceased to exist, God would not only notice, he would be devastated. Yes, he loves you that much. He is the almighty creator of heaven and earth. He lacks nothing and yet he desires you. Rather than consider how small you are, you would do much better to ask the question, "How big is God?" This Psalm answers that question.

If you sometimes wonder what your place is on this orb, then this Psalm is for you. If you feel isolated from the pack and an insignificant speck in a big world, then this is your Psalm. When you realize how big God is and yet how important you are to him, then you will begin to see your own place and significance in his creation.

***

Psalm 8

This psalm was designed to be sung and accompanied by a guitar. The theme is stated in the first verse and then repeated in the last verse:

> O LORD, our Lord, how majestic is your name in all the earth! You have set your glory above the heavens.

—Ps. 8:1

Literally this verse reads: "O LORD [Eternal One], our Lord [Master]..." His name is Eternal Master. Jesus earned that name on the cross:

> Who, being in very nature God, did not consider equality with God something to be grasped, but made himself nothing, taking the very nature of a servant, being made in human likeness. And being found in appearance as a man, he humbled himself and became obedient to death, even death on a cross! Therefore God exalted him to the highest place and gave him the name that is above every name, that at the name of Jesus every knee should bow, in heaven and on earth and under the earth, and every tongue confess that Jesus Christ is Lord, to the glory of God the Father.
>
> —Phil. 2:6-11

"You have set your glory above the heavens." The Lord's glory is not only seen in heaven, of course. On the contrary, the Bible is filled with references to how things on the earth point to God's glory, verses like: "Holy, holy, holy is the LORD Almighty; the whole earth is full of his glory" (Isa 6:3). This Psalm tells us that God's glory is higher than anything on the earth or in heaven. All things on the earth and in heaven were created by God and the glory of created things is merely a reflection of his glory. When God gave his law to the Jews, defining his relationship with them, it was no accident that his first commandment was: "You shall have no other gods before me" (Ex. 20:3). God wants to have the very highest place in our lives. Anything that is higher than God is an idol.

"O LORD, our Lord, how majestic is your name in all the earth! You have set your glory above the heavens." I picture David writing this Psalm. I imagine him thinking back to his boyhood shepherding days, reflecting on the many nights he spent alone with his sheep on the hillsides of Judea under the starlit heavens.

I have often been drawn to the creator by his creation. My family lived in Tucson, Arizona for a few years and I enjoyed solo hikes in the Santa Catalina Mountains. I recall one magnificent night on top of Mount Kimball. It was a clear, calm evening. I sat with my back against an ancient ponderosa pine and looked out over the glimmering lights of Tucson spread below me and the twinkling points of millions of stars suspended above me. I reached the summit of the mountain in the quickening darkness as the sun set below an adjoining peek. Normally, I would have been busy setting up my tent and organizing the campsite in the fading daylight, but I found myself in an almost trance-like state as I leaned against the tree and beheld the glory of God literally unfolding before me. I don't know how long I sat there, having lost track of time, but God seemed so real and felt so close. As I remember that time, I imagine David, the shepherd boy, sitting on that Judean hillside penning these words: "O LORD, our Lord, how majestic is your name in all the earth! You have set your glory above the heavens."

God is so big, so glorious, and so majestic that he is beyond description. I'm convinced that this truth is totally essential to the Christian experience. I believe most of our problems stem from our small view of God. There are two truths that we must grasp. The first is that God loves us. The second is that God is big enough to take care of us in every circumstance. This is what the psalmist addresses here.

What if God were not approachable or you had no contact with him? What if God didn't love you, or wasn't strong enough to take care of you? David addresses these questions in verses two through eight:

> From the lips of children and infants you have ordained praise because of your enemies, to silence the foe and the avenger.
>
> —Ps. 8:2

In spite of God's greatness, his nature can still be grasped and expressed by children. David sat, pen in hand, and was challenged by his attempt to describe God; he couldn't. God is beyond the ability of language. And yet David knew that God reveals himself in such a way that even small children can know him. The psalmist's observation is confirmed by an incident in the New Testament:

> The blind and the lame came to [Jesus] at the temple, and he healed them. But when the chief priests and the teachers of the law saw the wonderful things he did and the children shouting in the temple area, "Hosanna to the Son of David," they were indignant. "Do you hear what these children are saying?" they asked him. "Yes," replied Jesus, "have you never read, 'From the lips of

> children and infants you have ordained praise?'"
>
> —Matt. 21:14-16

The chief priests and the teachers of the law didn't recognize their God; but the children knew. That little band of street urchins wasn't a children's choir. They hadn't been trained by the temple leaders. They were out of order. They weren't worshipping according to tradition or law. They were running and leaping in the house of God. How shocking to those who would choose proper over praise. Those rowdy little children had their hearts open. When Jesus came into the temple and healed the lame and the blind, it was the children that broke into spontaneous praise. I love the way the *New Living Bible* paraphrases this verse: "You have taught the little children to praise you perfectly. May their example shame and silence your enemies!" The priests and the teachers thought that Jesus should silence the rambunctious children; but the children were the ones who had caught the truth.

Paul re-confirmed this idea in first Corinthians:

> For Christ did not send me to baptize, but to preach the gospel — not with words of human wisdom, lest the cross of Christ be emptied of its power. For the message of the cross is foolishness to those who are perishing, but to us who are being saved it is the power of God. For it is written: "I will destroy the wisdom of the wise; the intelligence of the intelligent I will frustrate." Where is the wise man? Where is the scholar? Where is the philosopher of this age? Has not God made foolish the wisdom of the world? For since in the wisdom of God, the world through its wisdom did not know him, God was pleased through the foolishness of what was preached to save those who believe.
>
> —1 Cor. 1:17-21

God can only be explained in terms of love...never logic!

This also applies to God's Word. If you come to God's Word with an attitude of academia, thinking that you need to dissect it, learn it, or sit in judgment of it, then the pages of the book will be closed to you; you won't understand them. But if you come as a child, impressed by everything, not thinking you know the answers, but with a spirit of wonder and discovery, then the book will begin to speak volumes to you. "At that time Jesus said, 'I praise you, Father, Lord of heaven and earth, because you have hidden these things from the wise and learned, and revealed them to little children'" (Matt 11:25).

It's not that God is against knowledge. The more you know about God the more you will be able to appreciate him and love him. God is a God of truth and knowing his truth will set you free. The point here is that you will never know God or learn from him unless you come to him with the humble attitude of a little child. You must come to Jesus as a wide-eyed kid, jump on his lap, and cry daddy. If you come to him with that attitude, the words of his love letter will be opened to your heart and your understanding.

***

> When I consider your heavens, the work of your fingers, the moon and the stars, which you have set in place...
>
> —Ps. 8:3

David spent many nights under the stars watching his sheep. With no pollution or city lighting, the stars were brilliant. Can you relate to how a brilliant star-filled sky, a red sunrise, or a purple sunset can draw you to your creator? David felt a mixture of mystery and awe as he looked at the night sky. We are affected, as David was, thirty centuries later.

Now David faces the inevitable question that must present itself whenever we contemplate the greatness of God's creation.

> What is man that you are mindful of him,
> the son of man that you care for him?

—Ps. 8:4

This same question cries for an answer in our day. Who are we? Why are we here? What is our purpose? As tiny cogs in this vast universe, how can we have significance?

There are two world views today that speak to the significance of men and women. The first is called the "European Enlightenment." The "E.E." says there is no life beyond life here on earth; therefore life here is meaningless. Bertrand Russell, who is known as the high priest of humanism, was a product of this philosophy and he answers the question of man's significance from his dark perspective:

> The life of man is a long march through the night surrounded by invisible foes, tortured by weariness and pain, toward a goal that few can hope to reach and where none may tarry long. One by one as they march, our comrades vanish from our sight, seized by the silent orders of omnipotent death. Brief and powerless is man's life. On him and all his race the slow sure doom falls pitiless and dark. Blind to good and evil, reckless of destruction, omnipotent matter rolls on its relentless way. For man, condemned today to lose his dearest, tomorrow himself, to pass through the gate of darkness, it remains only to cherish the thoughts that ennoble this little day.

When people have no hope for a future, it warps their present. The fruit of the "European Enlightenment" was Nazism and Communism.

The other world view is called the "Asian Enlightenment." The "A.E." says that beyond this life is re-incarnation and that the ultimate goal of mankind is to climb to higher and higher life forms until a soul finally ceases to exist in Nirvana. There is no significance to life and the highest state a person can achieve is to cease to exist. The A.E. birthed the Hindu caste system and doomed over a billion people to insignificance in this time and an eternity separated from their creator.

These two philosophies are largely embraced by our world today and humanity is slowly sinking in the despair of insignificance. Both world views see life as worthless and hopeless.

But there is another world view — another enlightenment. There is the light of the world.

The Biblical world view is in direct contrast to other world views as the Psalm answers the question about the significance of man:

> You made him a little lower than the heavenly beings and crowned him with glory and honor.
>
> —Ps. 8:5

This verse is better translated by the *New American Standard* version of the Bible: "Yet

Thou hast made him a little lower than God..." The *Septuagint*, which is the Greek translation of the Old Testament, used the word "angels" but the original Hebrew word is Elohim...GOD! With this in mind, the Bible makes an outrageous statement. We have been created a little lower than God himself!

What an incredible difference between this and Bertrand Russell's world view. According to the Bible, men and women were created a little lower than their creator. They were made to be the expression of God's life, the means by which an invisible God would be made visible to creation. People are the instrument by which God will do his work in the world. We are the creature nearest to God. We are not just another member of the animal kingdom; we are unique. God's plan is that we will be the channel of his blessing to all creation. We represent the ultimate of his creativity. Each one of us represents God's very best work on his very best day. His plan is to glorify us, to lift each one of us up for eternity as the masterpiece of his creation. Talk about significance!

> You made him ruler over the works of your hands; you put everything under his feet: all flocks and herds, and the beasts of the field, the birds of the air, and the fish of the sea, all that swim the paths of the seas.
>
> —Ps. 8:6-8

"You made him ruler over the works of your hands." Is this true? Has God really put us over all he has made? Are we really in charge of stuff?

> Then God said, "Let us make man in our image, in our likeness, and let them rule over the fish of the sea and the birds of the air, over the livestock, over all the earth, and over all the creatures that move along the ground." So God created man in his own image, in the image of God he created him; male and female he created them. God blessed them and said to them, "Be fruitful and increase in number; fill the earth and subdue it. Rule over the fish of the sea and the birds of the air and over every living creature that moves on the ground."
>
> —Gen. 1:26-28

God gave complete dominion over his creation to Adam and Eve. But that dominion was conditional: "You must not eat from the tree of the knowledge of good and evil, for when you eat of it you will surely die" (Gen. 2:17).

> To Adam he said, "Because you listened to your wife and ate from the tree about which I commanded you, 'You must not eat of it,' "Cursed is the ground because of you; through painful toil you will eat of it all the days of your life. It will produce thorns and thistles for you, and you will eat the plants of the field. By the sweat of your brow you will eat your food until you return to the ground, since from it you were taken; for dust you are and to dust you will return."
>
> —Gen. 3:17-19

When Adam and Eve sinned, they lost their inheritance. Creation was no longer under their dominion. How then in Psalm 8 can David say that God has put everything under our feet?

I believe that David was writing prophetically. He was looking ahead to God's promise and plan for his people.

> And God placed all things under his [Christ's] feet and appointed him to be

> head over everything for the church, which is his body, the fullness of him who fills everything in every way.
>
> —Eph. 1:22-23

Today all of creation is under Christ's feet, the second Adam. And we are in Christ.

And so to tie all of this together:

> 1. We are so significant to God that he has placed us just below himself in glory.
>
> 2. God values us so much that when we fell from glory he sacrificed his own son to raise us up.
>
> 3. God has all the power in the universe and he has entrusted that power to us in his son.

God has placed Christ over everything — for the church.

What a magnificent God who created the infinite vastness of the universe and yet can be known by children. "O Lord, how can you be so big and still delight in me? How can it be that my intellect cannot begin to fathom you and yet you are sunshine to my heart? How can you be so infinite, so all in all, and yet I can call you father...even daddy. I sit at my desk today and cry. I bow my heart before you and tremble. You are my God, my Lord, and my Father. I reach up to take your hand today and accept your warm kiss."

> O LORD, our Lord, how majestic is your name in all the earth!
>
> —Ps. 8:9

Life Lesson

Knowing How Important You Are to God

Consider and discuss: How has meditating on this Psalm changed how you feel about yourself and your place in the universe?

How do you think God feels about you? Are you important to him? Why?

Name some things in nature that point to God's glory. Describe why these things bring glory to God. Contemplate or share how these things draw you to the creator.

God loves you and he is powerful enough to take care of you. Is that statement true? If so then can you trust God to be your protector? How does it make you feel knowing that the one who created the universe is watching after you?

Psalm 13

Hope for the Hopeless

Years ago I experienced one of the most stressful times of my life. I had worked for a company for about ten years and had advanced until I was a senior vice president. The corporate politics was fierce, with no lack of those who would like to see me fail. And fail I did. A major computer expansion stumbled and I found myself gripped with anxiety as I watched my job slowly crumble around me. I desperately tried to find a way out of the mess, but there was no escape. I lost hope. For over a year I watched the slow-motion demolition of what I thought was my life. I was a mess. "Where is God?" I asked myself many times during that terrible period.

We all have twenty-twenty vision when looking backward. I had no way of knowing at the time that God was busy during that terrible year ordering my future. I couldn't know that a failed job would lead to a very successful consulting career and many other blessings. If only I had known, I would not have lost hope.

Is there even such a thing as indestructible hope, a hope that is never crushed? Can we always trust God to come through for us? God has promised us that he will never leave or abandon us. We know that he is faithful and always interceding for his children; we know these things and yet stuff still happens. "Where is God?" is a phrase that often crosses our consciousness. How does God work? Is he a friend who shows up from time-to-time and helps us with our problems and then just goes away and ignores us for periods of time, or is he a friend that is always with us to either rescue us from trouble, or stand with us in it?

Or is Baal your God? What! What kind of question is that! You know — Baal — the false god of the Israelites during the long ago days of King Ahab. Do you remember the story? The Israelites had begun worshipping Baal, the storm god, because they believed he could help them provide timely rain for their crops. After all, Baal was considered to be the god who could control the weather. He was god of rain and sun. He could bring good weather or stormy, depending on whether or not you were in his favor. He was thought to be a powerful god who could send fire and thunder falling from heaven. There were few in that day who had not worshipped Baal. The worship of the Lord was in decline, but there was one man who stood up for Jehovah, the prophet Elijah. It's a great story. It climaxes with Elijah challenging all the prophets of Baal to a test in order to determine who was truly God. They each constructed an altar of sacrifice and then prayed to their god to light the fire. The prophets of Baal went first:

> So they took the bull given them and prepared it. Then they called on the name of Baal from morning till noon. "O Baal, answer us!" they shouted. But there was no response; no one answered. And they danced around the altar they had made.
>
> —1 Kings 18:26

They danced around the altar but there was no response; no one answered. Elijah mocked them for believing in a false god:

> At noon Elijah began to taunt them. "Shout louder!" he said. "Surely he is a god! Perhaps he is deep in thought, or busy, or traveling. Maybe he is sleeping and must be awakened."
>
> —1 Kings 18:27

So in the middle of your struggle, where is God; is he busy or traveling? Is he like Baal? Does he show up occasionally and is not to be found at other times? Think about your perception of God. Will he be there for you in those times when you need help? If you want your hope to be indestructible, you have to hope in the God who is. Hoping in the God of your expectations will not serve you well.

Psalm 13 helps us discover the "God who is."

***

Psalm 13

This Psalm expresses the deep anguish of a troubled heart. Although a personal enemy is behind the scenes, the psalmist's primary distress is with his own doubts about God. The Psalm is divided into three sections of two verses each. It traces David's mental journey from hoping in the God of his expectations, to hoping in the God who is.

The Psalm follows David on a metaphorical heart passage from flat on his face, to his knees, and eventually to his feet. He travels from doubt and hopelessness and eventually arrives, confident that his help is from the Lord. He traverses from believing in the God of his perception to the God he believes in by faith.

Six verses monitor David's trek:

David on his face:

> How long, O LORD? Will you forget me forever? How long will you hide your face from me? How long must I wrestle with my thoughts and every day have sorrow in my heart? How long will my enemy triumph over me?
>
> —Ps. 13:1-2

David on his knees:

> Look on me and answer, O LORD my God. Give light to my eyes, or I will sleep in death; my enemy will say, "I have

overcome him," and my foes will rejoice when I fall.

—Ps. 13:3-4

David on his feet:

> But I trust in your unfailing love; my heart rejoices in your salvation. I will sing to the LORD, for he has been good to me.

—Ps. 13:5-6

David used the phrase "How long?" four times in the first two verses. Apparently he had been in turmoil for a long time. God had been silent. Do you make the journey from face, to knees, and eventually, to feet or do you get stuck in the "How long?" frame of mind and stay on your face?

David was an emotional man with many internal struggles. He battled with his thoughts and with the awesome responsibility of leadership. His failures in his family and the constant pursuit of his enemies made him a man of sorrow. He was wearied by his enemy but even more distressed by God's seeming unconcern. He felt that in the time of his greatest need God had abandoned him.

The question of perceived abandonment puzzles us all at one time or another. Which of us can say there haven't been times when we've felt alone? Why does God sometimes not answer and what do you do when God doesn't seem to respond to your need? What did David do?

David went to his knees:

> Look on me and answer, O LORD my God. Give light to my eyes, or I will sleep in death; my enemy will say, "I have overcome him," and my foes will rejoice when I fall.
>
> —Ps. 13:3-4

By "give light to my eyes," David is asking the Lord to put a sparkle back in his eyes. He is also asking God to give him clarity, that he might know the purpose for his suffering.

The Psalm doesn't tell us how David progressed from his face to his knees and then back on his feet, but it is clear in verses five and six that David's prayer was answered. God did indeed put a sparkle back in his eyes.

> But I trust in your unfailing love; my heart rejoices in your salvation. I will sing to the LORD, for he has been good to me.
>
> —Ps. 13:5-6

How has David's outlook changed? I doubt that his circumstances have improved from verse four to five. A careful re-reading of the Psalm reveals that David's thoughts have made a transition, and that a change in focus has restored his hope. Notice in verses one to four that David's entire attention is on himself and his problems. "How long will you forget *me* Lord?" "How long must *I* wrestle with *my* thoughts?" "Answer *me* Lord." "Give light to *my* eyes." In David's mind it is all about him and his situation. He is totally engrossed in those problems and he sees the Lord as an external force that should be helping him.

Now look at verses 5-6. Something has drastically changed. David's problems are no longer front and center in his mind but now he has shifted his heart to the Lord. "I trust in *your* unfailing love." "My heart rejoices in *your* salvation." "I will sing to the Lord, *he* has been good to me."

David's experience is not unique in the Bible. Jeremiah, the prophet, experienced some of the same struggles. He was known as the "weeping prophet" because of his many hardships. He was the major prophet during the decline and fall of the southern Jewish kingdom of Judah. Let's examine Jeremiah's life looking for principles that will help us live with genuine hope.

God called Jeremiah and appointed him to be Israel's prophet. Jeremiah was God's spokesman. Literally hundreds of verses in the book of Jeremiah begin with, "The word of the Lord came to me." But Jeremiah was not a happy man; his destiny was to be a prophet of doom. Like all Jews, he loved Jerusalem. God has put a special love for Jerusalem into the heart of every Jew since he first promised the land to Abraham. God gave Jeremiah a life ministry of warning the people of God's judgment and the destruction of Jerusalem because of their Baal worship. He was stuck with a ministry of negativity and was persecuted for his politically incorrect preaching. You think your life is tough. Jeremiah spent his whole life between a rock and a hard place and things were so bad that eventually he came to the conclusion that God's calling on his life was actually a curse.

Imagine spending your whole life praying, preaching, and hoping for a people who would not listen, only to see them crushed and their holy city destroyed. These verses pretty much sum up how he felt:

> Cursed be the day I was born! May the day my mother bore me not be blessed! Cursed be the man who brought my father the news, who made him very glad, saying, "A child is born to you — a son!" May that man be like the towns the LORD overthrew without pity. May he hear wailing in the morning, a battle cry at noon. For he did not kill me in the womb, with my mother as my grave, her womb enlarged forever. Why did I ever come out of the womb to see trouble and sorrow and to end my days in shame?
>
> —Jer. 20:14-18

Jeremiah served the Lord and the people of Israel for 40 years and eventually came to the place where he had no hope. One of the things I plan on doing when I get to heaven is to look up Jeremiah and see if things are going better for him. "Having a good forever Jer?" I already know what his answer will be. And he didn't have to wait to get to heaven. God didn't use Jeremiah at Jeremiah's expense. He never does that. Through it all, Jeremiah learned the meaning of genuine hope. In fact, he became a man of indestructible hope.

And through Jeremiah's experience, God teaches us the meaning of genuine hope. Hope is not a longing or yearning for God to act on our behalf. Hope is not just waiting for the slim chance that things may get better. Genuine hope is the confidence that God is in our life, now and forever, and that nothing can separate us from his love.

True hope is resting in the unending love of your creator, expecting him to act on your behalf.

Don't ever forget that God is for you. Lamentations chapter three charts Jeremiah's descent into hopelessness and his ascent to real hope. It expresses his journey from focusing on self to resting in God. In the following verses as Jeremiah recounts his woes, notice his use of personal pronouns:

> *I am* the man who has seen affliction by the rod of his wrath. He has driven *me*

away and made *me* walk in darkness rather than light; indeed, he has turned his hand against *me* again and again, all day long. He has made *my skin* and *my flesh* grow old and has broken *my* bones. He has besieged *me* and surrounded *me* with bitterness and hardship. He has made *me* dwell in darkness like those long dead. He has walled *me* in so *I* cannot escape; he has weighed *me* down with chains. Even when *I* call out or cry for help, he shuts out *my* prayer. He has barred *my way* with blocks of stone; he has made *my paths* crooked. Like a bear lying in wait, like a lion in hiding, he dragged *me* from the path and mangled *me* and left *me* without help. He drew his bow and made *me* the target for his arrows. He pierced my heart with arrows from his quiver. *I* became the laughingstock of all *my people*; they mock *me* in song all day long. He has filled *me* with bitter herbs and sated *me* with gall. He has broken my teeth with gravel; he has trampled *me* in the dust. *I* have been deprived of peace; *I* have forgotten what prosperity is. So *I* say, "*My* splendor is gone and *all that I had hoped from the LORD.*" *I* remember *my* affliction and *my* wandering, the bitterness and

> the gall. *I* well remember them, and *my* soul is downcast within me.
>
> —Lam 3:1-20 (italics mine)

Phew! It wears me out. Just reading the "weeping prophet" makes me want to curl up in the fetal position.

Jeremiah had hoped that the people would wake up and be saved. It never happened. Like most of us who have hoped that God would accomplish our vision, Jeremiah ended up questioning and finally blaming the Lord. Jeremiah was alone, rejected by his people, and now it seemed, even God.

Verse eighteen was the breaking point for Jeremiah. Good thing. God was cracking Jeremiah open to let "self" drain out so the Lord could fill the prophet with himself. The prophet was being broken open so that God could fill him with the kind of hope that only comes as a gift from God.

In the midst of his anguish, a laser beam of truth penetrated the dungeon of Jeremiah's mind. In the depths of despair, a gift was given and the gift was the giver.

> Yet this I call to mind and therefore I have hope: because of the LORD's great

> love we are not consumed, for his compassions never fail. They are new every morning; great is your faithfulness. I say to myself, "The LORD is my portion; therefore I will wait for him."

> —Lam. 3:21-24

"The LORD is my portion; therefore I will wait for him." The prophet emerges from his dark night with four great convictions that lead to a liberating experience of indestructible hope:

1. "Because of the Lord's great love, we are not consumed." God's judgment is always coupled with the possibility of a new beginning. God specializes in new beginnings; he is the God of new beginnings. It's who he is. It's what he does: "For I know the plans I have for you," declares the LORD, "plans to prosper you and not to harm you, plans to give you hope and a future. Then you will call upon me and come and pray to me, and I will listen to you. You will seek me and find me when you seek me with all your heart" (Jer. 29:11-13).

God was not finished with his chosen people or with his appointed prophet and he isn't finished with you or me.

2. "...for his compassions never fail." Jeremiah realized that God would never give up on him or his people. And we have seen more of God's mercy than Jeremiah. We have the incarnation, the cross, the resurrection, and Pentecost. Christ defeated sin on the cross and death on Easter morning. These events alone should replace meager hope with living hope.

3. "They are new every morning, great is your faithfulness." Hope is reborn daily. Mercy flows fresh from the throne of God and it is not dependent on our perfection, or our preparedness, but God's faithfulness. Mercy comes when we least deserve it.

4. "The Lord is my portion." The gift is the giver. Jeremiah had moved from wanting the Lord to act on his behalf to just wanting the Lord period.

***

New Testament perspective:

Peter:

> Praise be to the God and Father of our Lord Jesus Christ! In his great mercy he has given us new birth into a living hope through the resurrection of Jesus Christ from the dead...
>
> —1 Pet. 1:3

Peter went through the same evolution as David and Jeremiah. Peter's hopes were pinned on his expectations of Jesus, but Calvary dashed those hopes. The living Lord of the resurrection filled Peter's broken heart with a new, imperishable hope, not based on expectations, but on the character of Christ.

As children of the King, we also have a new hope. Ditch the world's fragile hope, where you may be, at best, optimistic about the possibilities. Embrace God's new hope, where you know that he is for you. Your new hope will not disappoint you because God has poured out his love into your heart by the Holy Spirit.

Learn the lesson from the psalmist, Jeremiah, and Peter. When trouble comes, learn the key to durable hope. Take the focus off yourself and place your future in God. He has glorious things in store for you.

> To them God has chosen to make known among the Gentiles the glorious riches of this mystery, which is Christ in you, the hope of glory.
>
> — Col. 1:27

Life Lesson

Knowing a hope that can never be crushed

Consider and discuss: How has meditating on this Psalm changed how you feel about yourself and your place in the universe?

Can you always trust God to come through for you in a crisis? Why or why not? Is your God someone who shows up occasionally and is not to be found at other times? What are your expectations of him?

Who or what do you sometimes place your trust in instead of the Lord?

David on his face: Can you think of a time where you felt as David — "How long, O LORD? Will you forget me forever?"

David on his knees: Do you pray and ask God to answer when you are in a crisis. Do you do it right away or is it a last resort?

David on his feet: Can you think of a time where you can praise the Lord that he has helped you in a crisis?

Psalm 23

Hope for Lost Lambs

Most Christians have read Psalm 23 many times. Some of us memorized it as children. It's probably been preached on more than any other passage of scripture. Even those who aren't really into the Bible know about the 23rd Psalm. And yet it is a rare and wonderful thing to read the Psalm all over again as if for the very first time, only this time experiencing it in a new way, doing our best to insert ourselves into the story and to experience the emotions of the story teller.

Psalm 23 is a great Psalm. It ministers to our deepest spiritual needs. It was written by David. You know David — shepherd, slinger, harpist, poet, soldier and king. It is no accident that David wrote most of the Psalms. The Psalms help us know the heart of God and God himself called David "a man after my own heart." David was an unusual mix; he was a warrior/poet.

To enter into David's feelings as he penned these famous verses, we have to know and understand his circumstances. For that we start in the Old Testament book of second Samuel:

> Then Absalom (David's son) sent secret messengers throughout the tribes of Israel to say, "As soon as you hear the sound of the trumpets, then say, 'Absalom is king in Hebron.'" Two hundred men from Jerusalem had accompanied Absalom. They had been invited as guests and went quite innocently, knowing nothing about the matter. While Absalom was offering sacrifices, he also sent for Ahithophel the Gilonite, David's counselor, to come from Giloh, his hometown. And so the conspiracy gained strength, and Absalom's following kept on increasing. A messenger came and told David, "The hearts of the men of Israel are with Absalom." Then David said to all his officials who were with him in Jerusalem, "Come! We must flee, or none of us will escape from Absalom.
>
> —2 Sam. 15:10-14

Maybe we should back up a little. David was the king. Even though he was a man after God's own heart, the Bible records his life as filled with sin and scandal. There was a lot of dirty linen hanging all over in the castle. David's family was torn by infidelity, lust, incest and rape. His relationship with his son Absalom was strained. Even though the Bible says David loved his son very much, there was an unexplained separation between them, and David grieved over their lack of mutual understanding. The scripture tells of one two-year period where David and Absalom never spoke to each other. And now Absalom has conspired to steal the throne from his father and the people have given their allegiance to Absalom. David was an emotional man. Can you imagine the hurt, anxiety, and even anger? Can you feel the bitterness trying to creep into his spirit?

***

Psalm 23

David loved his son Absalom. Later he cried and grieved at his death. Imagine how he felt to have his own son trying to kill him. Imagine the turmoil that David went through. He has lost his kingdom, his son, and the love of the people. He has lost everything in his life that he cares about. He must have felt very much alone out in the wilderness where he had fled, the same wilderness where he had spent most of his time as a young shepherd. Imagine David as he sits down on a rock. His heart is broken. With swollen and tear filled eyes, he picks up a quill and he writes:

> The LORD is my shepherd; I shall not be in want.
>
> —Ps. 23:1

This is a Psalm for people who, like David, are experiencing major loss; it's for people who have been stunned by life. If your life has been shaken to its core, then this Psalm is for you. Or maybe you are not in turmoil right now. Then you need to have this Psalm with you and ready. Think of Psalm 23 as one of the tools of the Swiss Army Knife of Psalms. You need to keep it handy so it's there when you need it. We will see in this Psalm that God feeds us, leads us, and protects us when we are in trouble.

I know, and you know, that it is a long journey from what we know to really experiencing the peace of being comforted and cared for. We look at God's Word and we see and believe the truth, but sometimes it is hard to actually put those truths into reality in our lives. We believe with our heads but our hearts are still lost and alone. The sixteen inches from our head to our heart can be a long journey.

Hey, talk is cheap! It's one thing to read Psalm 23 and be warmed by the words, but what do you do when you are facing real trouble? Do you remember these things? I mean, let's be practical. Do these eternal truths really kick in and do they come to your aid? Do you find that God brings you his provision and his peace when you are faced with need? Does it work? Is this stuff real? Is there anything that we can take to the bank? Can we know that we know?

Francis Schaffer, a Christian theologian, was lecturing in a college when he was asked by some of the unbelieving students the question: "Why are you a Christian?" They were all sitting with pen and paper waiting for a great philosophical or theological explanation, an apologetic renunciation of everything else, and a defense of Christendom. Do you know what he said? He said, "I am a Christian because it is the truth."

It's not very popular in the world today but Jesus is the truth. He is the only truth. It's not politically correct for me to say this, but there are no other beliefs that we need to acknowledge or respect. We should respect all people, but if they do not worship the one true God they are not living in the truth.

So it is of no value for us as Christians to grapple with the truth. That isn't going to be helpful for us. Our duty isn't to grapple with the truth but to live it, to bring our lives in line with it.

I think it is probably a fair statement that many of us, me included, sometimes find it very difficult to put the truths of Psalm 23 into practice in our lives. I think sometimes we need help, some assurance of God's presence, a guarantee that he will be there for us when we go through struggles.

Maybe as he writes this Psalm the psalmist is saying in his heart, "How can I know?

How can I really know that he will be with me in this terrible time?" Just like David, we need to speak the truth and then trust the Savior to confirm it by revealing it to our hearts.

And so, in his anguish and doubt, David speaks the truth in faith: "The LORD is my shepherd; I shall not be in want." This is cause and effect. Because the Lord is my shepherd, therefore there is nothing I lack. Is the Lord your shepherd? If the Lord is your shepherd, then you lack nothing. Okay, some of you just hit the pause button. You are thinking about your life and you are not entirely satisfied. You are in want; you lack. Does that mean the Lord is not your shepherd?

There are really only two options in life. There are two groups of people; you belong to one group or the other. Those in the first group are those who can say, "The Lord is my Shepherd; therefore I shall not be in want." Everyone else is in group two. They say "I am in want; therefore the Lord is not my shepherd."

Is it really that simple? Yes. If there is emptiness and loneliness and frustration in your life, then at that point the Lord is not your shepherd. If anyone or anything else besides the Lord shepherds you, you will not be satisfied. If your job shepherds you, you will be restless, unfulfilled and frustrated. If education is your shepherd, you will be disillusioned. If drugs or alcohol are your shepherd, you will be wasted. If you depend on family or friends or church or possessions to shepherd you, then you will be needy, powerless, disappointed and angry.

This is the place where God wants to bring us. He wants us to be dependent on him and only him. Don't despair if you look at your life and have to admit that you are in group two, that you are in need. David considered himself in group two but he was practicing a little self-talk by saying that the Lord was his shepherd and therefore he wasn't going to be in need. He was in this first verse declaring that by an act of his will he was going to count himself in group one, even though he didn't feel that way at the moment. Sometimes when we are not where we want and need to be, we can begin to move by just declaring that we are going to trust him to take care of us.

Now there is a problem. If the Lord is your shepherd, what are you? You are a sheep. Great! How does that make you feel? Sheep are just about the dumbest animals on the face of the earth. On the smart-scale, sheep come in just after night crawlers. Why do you think the Lord so often uses the analogy of shepherd/sheep when he is talking about his relationship with us? What is it about sheep that makes them a good representation of who we are? Well, they wander off and they don't know what's good for them. They lack wisdom and strength. They are self-destructive. The Bible says: "We all, like sheep, have gone astray; each of us has turned to his own way..." (Isa 53:6). It's not very encouraging, but I guess when you think about it we are a lot like sheep.

The shepherd's job is to keep the sheep together, to keep them fed, to keep them safe, and to keep them from wandering off. When a particular lamb would continually wander off, the shepherd would break its leg as a way of protecting it. Then he would carry it. How does that picture make you feel about your relationship with your shepherd? How does that picture affect how you feel about that part of you that's broken? You know, when the shepherd picks up that little lamb with the broken leg, it just snuggles itself in his arms. It isn't angry or afraid. It doesn't blame the shepherd. It doesn't know why the shepherd broke its leg, but it does know how much the shepherd loves it and it trusts its protector. The lamb never questions the love of the shepherd. It has experienced the shepherd's loving care and watched as he fought off the wolf. The lamb knows that the shepherd would lay down his life for the sheep; he feels safe in the presence of the shepherd. Wow! I guess sheep are very smart in the things that count!

Okay, so if the Lord is my shepherd and if a shepherd's task is to meet the needs of the sheep, then how does God meet my needs?

> He makes me lie down in green pastures...

—Verse 2a

The picture here is of sheep bedded down in a grassy meadow having eaten their fill. They are content and at rest. The idea for us is that if God is our shepherd then he will meet the needs of our inner man. Our spirits will be at rest and content. Is that the way David was feeling when he wrote these words? I don't think so. His spirit was in turmoil. Did he really believe what he was writing? Just like the sheep with the broken leg, he was resting in his master's arms by faith. It's the same for us. We can have peace and comfort right in the middle of the storms of life if we will learn to rest in him. In him, we find the soft and quiet "green pastures" of content.

> ...he leads me beside quiet waters.
>
> —Verse 2b

Sheep are afraid of running water. They will only drink from a quiet pool. A good shepherd would never lead his flock to drink from flowing water. Jesus knows what you are afraid of and if the Lord is your shepherd he will lead you to the quiet, safe place where you can drink and have your thirst satisfied.

> ...he restores my soul.
>
> —Verse 3a

What does it mean to have the Good Shepherd restore your soul? He is the creator of life. He is the one who created your soul. Literally, he will cause "life" to flow into you. The word "restore" here is important. The sheep eat the tender green shoots and are satisfied. They quench their thirst from the quiet pool and their life is renewed. It's the same for us. No matter our circumstance, God has provided that we should be at rest and satisfied. No matter what we are going through in our lives God wants to restore our souls. How do you respond in times of stress and turmoil? What is your response when life doesn't go well? Do you feel that God has let you down by allowing this thing in your life or do you feel like you have let God down by not trusting when things go wrong? Jesus said: "I am the Good Shepherd; I know my sheep" (John 10:14). He knows you. He knows your weakness. He doesn't condemn you for not trusting but he wants to "restore your soul." He wants to lift you above your troubles. "Therefore we do not lose heart." "Though outwardly we are wasting away, yet inwardly we are being renewed day by day" (2 Cor 4:16). Our food is the Word of God. As we feed on it, God's Word brings us rest and peace and renewal.

> ...He guides me in paths of righteousness for his name's sake.
>
> —Verse 3b

The shepherd meets our needs and heals our emotions. He will also lead us and show us his path. The Hebrew word here translated "paths" means "well-worn track." But if we have a well-worn track to follow why do we need a guide? If you are thinking this way that's because you have forgotten that you are a sheep. No matter how obvious the path is, sheep are still inclined to wander off and get lost.

When my wife Barb and I were in our twenties, we lived for a few years in Tucson Arizona. I loved going backpacking with my friend Frank in the Santa Catalina Mountains. On one of our many treks, we were climbing up into one of the steep canyons headed toward a mountain peak when we overtook another hiker. He was an elderly gentleman and he had an aluminum hiking stick. Frank and I passed him quickly, and as soon as we were out of earshot of the man we began laughing. We mocked him for climbing this steep pass at his advanced age (he was probably fifty) and for the comical click, click, click of his aluminum pole as he slowly made his way along. At the pace he was going we figured that we would probably see him again about half way up as we were on our way down. Further up the pass, Frank and I looked far ahead and we could see the trail a long way off. Scanning the terrain ahead, we decided there was a faster way to get where we were going than simply following the trail. Planning to intersect the trail several miles ahead we began bushwhacking cross-country. Several hours later found us hopelessly lost and sweaty, low on water and spirit. We laid down at the bottom of a small gully trying to decide what our next step would be. We had no idea where we were or which way to go. I've been on many backpacking journeys with Frank but I think it was this trip where I began using that famous line from Laurel and Hardy — "Just another fine mess you've gotten me into!" As we lay in that little gully pondering our fate, we suddenly heard a familiar and steadily louder sound... click, click, click. "Oh no! It's the old man with the aluminum walking stick!" We hunkered down low so he wouldn't see us as he slowly clicked his way past us on the trail at the top of the little ditch where we lay. After he had passed us and turned a bend, we climbed the fifteen feet to the trail that a minute before we didn't even know was there. We followed the trail from then on and we had to walk slower because we were too embarrassed to pass him again. "We all, like sheep, have gone astray, each of us has turned to his own way..." (Isa 53:6). Baa.

The path of righteousness truly is a well-worn track. We know the way. None of us will miss the prize out of ignorance. And yet we often stray from the path. Sometimes we stray because God's way doesn't seem to make sense. Sometimes we wander off the track following our own lusts. Sometimes we just want to have it our own way. Think about it. You are a sheep. We all are. The Bible says that each of us has turned to his own way. Every one of us is a rebellious child wanting what we want. But the shepherd knows the path and he doesn't give up on wayward sheep. He never abandons sheep because they stray. He loves them all the same. He's been down the trail before. The sheep need to learn to trust him. We don't know what calamity the next bend in the path will bring us. Do you find it difficult to trust the shepherd with your future? As we project what "could" happen in the future, our minds are filled with all kinds of foreboding possibilities, and we are faced with decisions every day that will ultimately shape our lives. We need wisdom. We need a shepherd, someone who knows the trail, someone who knows what lies ahead and someone we can trust. "Your word is a lamp to my feet and a light for my path" (Ps. 119:105).

So the Lord knows the way. But the question that often comes up is how can I discover God's way for my life? How does the sheep know what the shepherd's will is? The shepherd would never yell at the sheep or bark out commands? No, his voice is quiet and peaceful, sometimes a mere whisper. The sheep always hear his directions for them because they are listening for his voice. When we learn to listen for the shepherd's voice, to follow him, then we will be on the path of his will. Sometimes our fears are too loud; sometimes our own thoughts drown out his voice. If we are going to know his way for us we are going to need to get quiet. The shepherd doesn't point the way, he leads the way. The only way for us to find his will is to follow him, listen to him, and read his love letter, the Bible, expecting to hear his voice. We should pray expecting him to answer. God said he would be our guide along the path. It's a promise. He said he will do it for the sake of His name. He must do it. His reputation, his character, his name is on the line. "I will lead the blind by ways they have not known, along unfamiliar paths I will guide them; I will turn the darkness into light before them and make the rough places smooth. These are the things I will do; I will not forsake them" (Isa 42:16).

The shepherd provides for the needs of the sheep, he restores their emotions, he guides them, and he also protects them.

> Even though I walk through the valley of the shadow of death, I will fear no evil, for you are with me
>
> —verse 4a

The scene here is of the shepherd leading the sheep through a narrow gorge late in the afternoon. This is the valley of deep shadows. The sheep are so timid and defenseless that they are afraid of their own shadows. But they trust the shepherd and as long as they can see him they are comforted. They are in a scary place but they fear no evil because they are with the shepherd and he will lead them through. "Be strong and courageous. Do not be afraid or terrified because of them, for the LORD your God goes with you; he will never leave you nor forsake you" (Deut 31:6). "No one will be able to stand up against you all the days of your life. As I was with Moses, so I will be with you; I will never leave you nor forsake you" (Josh 1:5).

David was able to pass this truth on to his son: "David also said to Solomon his son, "Be strong and courageous, and do the work. Do not be afraid or discouraged, for the LORD God, my God, is with you. He will not fail you or forsake you until all the work for the service of the temple of the LORD is finished" (1 Chr 28:20).

How can we be sure that our shepherd is always with us? We can be sure because he said he would be. "But now, this is what the LORD says—he who created you, O Jacob, he who formed you, O Israel: "Fear not, for I have redeemed you; I have summoned you by name; you are mine. When you pass through the waters, I will be with you; and when you pass through the rivers, they will not sweep over you. When you walk through the fire, you will not be burned; the flames will not set you ablaze" (Isa 43:1-2).

Maybe you've had a "valley of the shadow" experience, a time when fear gripped you and paralyzed you. When I was about ten years old I was swimming at the beach with my family. I decided to swim under a dock and come out the other side. I went through the one side but I hit my head on one of the support bars when I tried to come out the other side. I tried again but still couldn't get through. I didn't think to open my eyes but just panicked and began thrashing around trying to find a way out. In my thrashing I reached out and found my father's hand, who realizing I was in trouble, had reached under the dock for me. I remember thinking to myself, "This won't do any good. I am hopelessly caught and he won't be able to pull me out because I don't fit through the bars." He pulled me out without even touching one of the bars because he had the right perspective of my difficulty.

When you take hold of your shepherd's hand, then you must trust him. His perspective is better than yours and he will pull you to safety.

> ...your rod and your staff, they comfort me.
>
> —verse 4b

The shepherd has a rod and a staff. The rod is for the outside enemy. God uses the rod to smash Satan's influence in your life. The staff is for the enemy within. He uses the staff to chasten us and keep us from wandering off. Both the rod and the staff are meant to comfort us. How do you respond when God disciplines you? Do you respond with anger or fear or do you nestle in his arms and be comforted. It's very humbling, but we need to learn from the sheep.

In the last two verses David changes the metaphor from shepherd to gracious host.

> You prepare a table before me in the presence of my enemies. You anoint my head with oil; my cup overflows.
>
> —verse 5

This new picture encompasses all the elements of the first picture. The fact that God feeds, provides, leads and protects is all bound up in this symbol of a gracious host. We all have an enemy that is out to destroy us. How disheartening it must be for our enemy to see us dining at the King's table. Paul said it this way: "And my God will meet all your needs according to his glorious riches in Christ Jesus" (Phil 4:19).

> Surely goodness and love will follow me all the days of my life.
>
> —verse 6a

The word "follow" here means to pursue, to chase after. God is pursuing you, chasing you, searching for you. Psalm 139 gives us a wonderful picture of how God never fails to pursue us. "O Lord, you have searched me and you know me. You know when I sit and when I rise; you perceive my thoughts from afar. You discern my going out and my lying down; you are familiar with all my ways. Before a word is on my tongue you know it completely, O Lord. You hem me in — behind and before; you have laid your hand upon me. Such knowledge is too wonderful for me, too lofty for me to attain" (Ps 139:1-6).

God is your creator. He knows you. He knows everything about you. How does it make you feel knowing that He sees it all, every action, every thought? Okay, we won't go there. Psalm 139 says that God is searching us. What does that mean? If he is our creator and he knows everything there is to know about us, then what exactly is he searching? Is this a positive thing or is he looking for sin? What exactly is he looking for? Does the word "search" scare you a little? In the original language the word "search" literally means, "to examine intimately, to penetrate, to mine or dig." The word was used as a mining term. It means literally, "to dig." Lord, you dig me! This means God understands us. You can never tell God that he doesn't understand you. He knows every last detail. There is nothing inside or outside of you that escapes His notice, and he still digs you.

He digs you!

The Father wants to get to the very bottom of you. He wants to dig through the pride, mine out the self-centeredness, shovel out the hurt and scrape clean the scars. He wants to empty you of every last thing that wasn't his idea and then fill the emptiness with the love of a God who has died for the sheep. He digs you! What does God find as

He searches your heart today? Have you given Him the mining rights?

While you were still a sinner Christ died for you. God is chasing you down to feed you, to provide all your needs, to guide you in the way everlasting, to protect you from your enemies. Way before you loved God he loved you enough to die for you. How do we respond to a God like this? We worship him. There is no other logical response to a God who would love like this. "We love because he first loved us" (1 John 4:19).

God is so good to us, so trustworthy, so loving.

> Surely goodness and love will follow me all the days of my life, and I will dwell in the house of the LORD forever.
>
> —verse 6

Life Lesson

___

Knowing God's tender care when we feel lost

Consider and discuss: Is the Lord your shepherd? Are all your needs met? Explain.

Discuss the ways that the Lord meets your needs.

Do you believe that the Lord will always be with you in times of trouble? How can you know for sure? Discuss.

The shepherd has a rod and a staff. The rod is for the outside enemy. God uses the rod to smash Satan's influence in your life. The staff is for the enemy within. He uses the staff to chasten us and keep us from wandering off. Both the rod and the staff are meant to comfort us. How do you respond when God uses his staff on you? Can you think of a time when God disciplined you? How did you react?

How does it make you feel knowing that you are going to spend an eternity with Jesus?

Psalm 40

Hope for the Shattered

I have been making annual mission trips to India since 2002. I have to admit looking back that in the beginning I was drawn to the place more by my love for adventure than my passion for souls. The passion for souls came as I sensed the spiritual darkness of the place and began to see the hunger and desperation of the beautiful people of India. I started by going with an interpreter, hanging out in remote villages and just making friends and talking to people about Jesus, The One True God. After several trips, the local church leadership convinced me to have open air Gospel festival meetings where I could speak to more people and introduce them to the God of love in a more efficient way. Since then the ministry has grown exponentially. Village to Village Ministries, a non-profit corporation, was formed in 2007 when I started bringing teams to India. Over the years Village To Village has watched God change hearts. Over 40,000 Hindus have made decisions to follow Jesus, four church buildings have been constructed in remote places and filled with new believers, and 22 fresh water wells have been bored in villages that before had no source of pure water. Every year we return home filled with stories of changed hearts and healed bodies, minds, and emotions.

Hotel accommodations are tough in the remote areas, but we always find something. One hotel gave us the solution to minimizing bed bug bites by keeping the lights on, since bed bugs only come out at night. Good to know.

One year in Krishna District we had some trouble with the Rashtriya Swayasevak Sangh (RSS). They are a powerful and sometimes militant Hindu organization that hates foreigners, Christians, and other races. Being a white Christian from America pretty much puts me on the top of their list. Our national team had some young men working security for the evening open-air Gospel festival that is attended by thousands of villagers. Usually we have the police helping us, but in Krishna District the RSS are the dominant political force. On our second night of preaching the police came and shut us down just before the altar call. There was nothing we could do but let our Indian crusade director deal with them. We went back to our hotel to pray. The next night they told us we could have the meeting but that no white person would be allowed on the stage. They told me to preach on the ground in front of the stage. I couldn't see the people from that vantage and didn't see how I could preach without being able to somehow connect with the crowd. How could I preach an effective message and tell the people about Jesus if they couldn't see me. I imagined it would be like speaking to an empty room with little energy accompanying my words. I was devastated. We had spent thousands of dollars and many months planning this trip. My heart sank and I cried out to God. As I started to preach I felt compelled to walk toward the crowd. Soon I was walking back and forth across the aisles of people, drawing energy from them as I told them about the only God in the universe that loves them. I'm sure the sound man was working on an ulcer as I walked in front of huge speaker systems with my microphone. That night our altar was overflowing with hundreds who came to know Jesus. The last night of our meetings the local police chief came to talk to me. It turns out that he is a Christian. He told me the order to close down our meetings had come from the district (county); he was only obeying orders. He expressed how sorry he was and that he felt he had dishonored his American guests. He said the God of Wonders (his words) came to him in a dream and told him to fight for the meetings with his superiors. He did and he won. As he told me the story his eyes glistened with tears and his lips were turned up in a gigantic grin. Two unlikely brothers stood in that soccer field, hugged and praised God together.

***

Psalm 40

This Psalm was written for shattered people, people in crisis, to be sung as a poetic testimony of how God rescues us in times of need. It was undoubtedly written with some current circumstance, but it also speaks prophetically about a future rescue of God's people. The Holy Spirit spoke as David recorded his troubles and caused the psalmist to express truths that were beyond his experience. The ultimate fulfillment of this Psalm would come when the Messiah appeared on the earth. In a sense, it is our Lord's autobiography where He tells his own story. This Psalm does some heavy lifting; applying not only to a current situation but also prophesying of the coming savior. It also uncovers truths that apply to you and me. This Psalm is meant to assure us that God is with us as we face trials. It is for those times when we find ourselves in the dead-end cul-de-sacs of life.

The writer begins with the conclusion, telling us where he is, and then describes how he got there. He begins with a cry and a song:

> I waited patiently for the LORD; he turned to me and heard my cry. He lifted me out of the slimy pit, out of the mud and mire; he set my feet on a rock and

gave me a firm place to stand. He put a new song in my mouth, a hymn of praise to our God. Many will see and fear and put their trust in the LORD.

—Ps. 40:1-3

The "slimy pit" is a metaphor for Jesus' death and resurrection...and ours. Think about the kind of experiences you have had that might be described as a "slimy pit." There is something wonderful about the fact that the metaphor describing Jesus' death and resurrection, also applies to us. In His death, Jesus experienced every kind of pain and suffering that we may ever encounter. We can never tell God he doesn't understand what we are going through because he has been through it himself and more.

But Jesus says the Lord lifted him out of that pit and set his feet on a rock. This is a picture of the resurrection. How many people have ever been resurrected? Lazarus was resurrected, but he died again. Jesus was resurrected with a new body, and would never die again. In a sense, we were resurrected when we became Christians; raised from death to life.

The psalmist's response to being lifted out of the slimy pit: "He put a new song in my mouth, a hymn of praise to our God. Many will see and fear and put their trust in the LORD." Can you imagine the joy Jesus felt at his resurrection? I imagine he woke up in that tomb with a song on his lips. Maybe verses four and five are the words of that song:

> Blessed is the man who makes the LORD his trust, who does not look to the proud, to those who turn aside to false gods. Many, O LORD my God, are the wonders you have done. The things you planned for us no one can recount to you; were I to speak and tell of them, they would be too many to declare.
>
> —Ps. 40:4-5

This song has two elements. The first is the secret of how to be blessed; how to go from hopeless to happy. "Blessed [happy] is the man who makes the LORD his trust, who does not look to the proud, to those who turn aside to false gods." This verse holds the secret to slimy-pit rescues. Ask yourself, "What or who do I trust for my happiness?" Do you expect your job, family, or church to make you happy? Do you believe that possessions will make you happy?

One of the big lies today is that we have special power in ourselves to be whatever we want to be. But it's a futile search looking for that power within. God made us to be dependent on him, to be incomplete without him. Happy is the person who learns that secret. Don't believe the lie. Blessed is the person who flees to his God, who runs to him for protection. If you place your trust in the stock market you will be constantly checking your portfolio. If you place your trust in your job you will become a workaholic. If you place your trust in people, you will lose your friends and other relationships as you put pressure on them to meet your needs. But if you place your trust in Jesus, you will be listening for his voice because he is your only hope. If you don't have a fallback position, then you will be still and wait for his voice.

"Happy is the man who makes the Lord his trust."

The second element of this song is in verse five. "Many, O LORD my God, are the wonders you have done. The things you planned for us no one can recount to you; were I to speak and tell of them, they would be too many to declare." These aren't just words. This isn't theological stuff. This is truth. The good that God has planned for you is beyond your capacity to explore. "For I know the plans I have for you," declares the LORD, "plans to prosper you and not to harm you, plans to give you hope and a future" (Jer. 29:11). He really is "...able to do immeasurably more than all we ask or imagine, according to his power that is at work within us" (Eph. 3:20).

Now beginning with verse six there is a change in the Psalm. We have covered the conclusion, the resurrection, and now we have what led up to this experience.

> Sacrifice and offering you did not desire, but my ears you have pierced; burnt offerings and sin offerings you did not require. Then I said, "Here I am, I have come — it is written about me in the scroll. I desire to do your will, O my God; your law is within my heart."

—Ps. 40:6-8

This part of the Psalm seems a little strange at first. What was wrong with sacrifice and burnt offering? These are the things we can give God. What is it that God really wants? God says, "I'm not interested in what you can give me or any sacrifice you can make for me. What I want is to pierce your ear." What's up with that? To understand this we have to look to the Jewish law concerning servants or slaves:

> If you buy a Hebrew servant, he is to serve you for six years. But in the seventh year he shall go free without paying anything. If he comes alone, he is to go free alone; but if he has a wife when he comes, she is to go with him. If his master gives him a wife and she bears him sons or daughters, the woman and her children shall belong to her master, and only the man shall go free. But if the servant declares, "I love my master and my wife and children and do not want to go free," then his master must take him before the judges. He shall take him to the door or the doorpost and pierce his ear with an awl. Then he will be his servant for life.
>
> —Exod. 21:2-6

God doesn't want your sacrifice, isn't interested in your good works, and won't be impressed by your obedience. He isn't concerned with how often you go to church, how much money you give, or how well you obey the "rules" with your human effort. Frankly, when lined up with God's holiness, everything you have to offer God is like filthy rags to him. God doesn't want what you can give him; he wants YOU. He wants to hear the words from Exodus on your lips. "I love my master, I will not go free." Forget about being acceptable to God because of your work ethic. The age of sacrifice and offerings is over. This is the age of ownership.

Can you imagine the excitement in heaven when Jesus gave up his life to set humanity free?

> I proclaim righteousness in the great assembly; I do not seal my lips, as you know, O LORD. I do not hide your righteousness in my heart; I speak of your faithfulness and salvation. I do not conceal your love and your truth from the great assembly.
>
> —Ps. 40:9-10

God gave his son a task and a message. His task was to die for the sins of the world. His message was love. He came to tell us that in spite of all the despair, evil and strife in the world, in spite of our sin and failure, God loves us and is willing to demonstrate that love by providing a resurrection in our lives. Beginning with verse eleven we have the description of his suffering:

> Do not withhold your mercy from me, O LORD; may your love and your truth always protect me. For troubles without number surround me; my sins have overtaken me, and I cannot see. They are more than the hairs of my head, and my heart fails within me.
>
> —Ps. 40:11-12

How could he say, "My sins have overtaken me" when he was innocent? Jesus never sinned but he took on our sin. "God made him who had no sin to be sin for us, so that in him we might become the righteousness of God" (2 Cor. 5:21). "But he was pierced for our transgressions, he was crushed for our iniquities; the punishment that brought us peace was upon him, and by his wounds we are healed" (Isa. 53:5).

Psalms, The Sunrise of Hope

> Be pleased, O LORD, to save me; O LORD, come quickly to help me. May all who seek to take my life be put to shame and confusion; may all who desire my ruin be turned back in disgrace. May those who say to me, "Aha! Aha!" be appalled at their own shame. But may all who seek you rejoice and be glad in you; may those who love your salvation always say, "The LORD be exalted!"

—Ps. 40:13-16

I believe verse seventeen expresses the cry of Jesus as he hung on the cross.

> Yet I am poor and needy; may the Lord think of me. You are my help and my deliverer; O my God, do not delay.

—Ps. 40:17

This is also our plea as we wait for our deliverer. This is the Gospel message. What a tremendous story. You and I are living in a day when people are afraid of what the future holds. The problems facing the world seem hopeless. All the streets seem to dead-end these days. We see shattered lives all around us. All of this confirms that there is no hope for us apart from the Gospel of Jesus Christ, no other way out of the darkness. God pulled his son out of the slimy pit and now Jesus stands ready to pull you out. Jesus Christ is your only hope to find the kind of life that God intends for you. Place your trust in him today. His love and truth are reaching for you. Run to the hope that is Christ.

Life Lesson

God delights in being our rescuer

Consider and discuss: A "slimy pit" experience would be a time when you were in trouble and couldn't see a way out. No matter what you did you couldn't seem to escape. Can you think of and share a time when you were in a "slimy pit?"

In this Psalm Jesus says the Lord lifted him out of that pit and set his feet on a rock. This is a picture of the resurrection. How did the Lord lift you out of your pit?

In this Psalm the writer says, "Sacrifice and offering you did not desire, but my ears you have pierced." How does it make you feel knowing that God isn't interested in what you can give or do but he wants you; he wants ownership.

In this Psalm when Jesus says, "my sins have overtaken me," how does it make you feel knowing it was really your sins that caused him such agony?

Psalm 42-43

Hope for the Despondent

In 1984 I went through a very difficult time at work. A major computer conversion went badly and I was gripped with anxiety as I watched my career slowly crumble. For over a year I watched the slow-motion demolition of what I thought was my life. I taught adult Sunday school, encouraging others to trust God with their circumstances. I wish my testimony from that hard time was how I brought it all to Jesus, and had confidence that he would bring me through. The truth is that my spirit sank as I saw no way out of my predicament. I had been studying the Bible for years. God had given me a love for his Word, which should have sustained me during those terrible days. But I was so low that I found I couldn't even read the Bible. I knew that the answer to my depression was to immerse myself in the Bible; but the words just bounced off, rather than minister to my broken spirit. I was miserable. During those dark days, there was one verse that I was able to read, one verse to help me hang on: "Why are you downcast, O my soul? Why so disturbed within me? Put your hope in God, for I will yet praise him, my Savior and my God" (Ps. 42:5). I recited this verse over and over, but it was all I had. The rest of God's Word was closed to me. Of course God was faithful and at work, even in my own inability to connect with him. Eventually my problems did work out to my great advantage and to God's glory. Looking back I see God in it all, moving me from one faith adventure to the next, and today I do praise him. Psalm 42 and its companion Psalm 43 hold a very special place in my heart.

***

Psalm 42-43

> For the director of music. A maskil of the Sons of Korah.
>
> —Ps. 42 Prefix

This Psalm was written for the director of music. It was a song to be sung when the

Israelites worshipped. It was also a "maskil" or "teaching," so there is something to learn as we sing this song.

The first lesson comes right in the prefix. The sons of Korah were a family of Levitical singers. Korah was a great-grandson of Levi and is well known for his rebellion against Jehovah. He incited a rebellion against Moses and recruited 250 leaders of Israel; who all came to Moses and challenged his leadership. You can read the story in Numbers chapter sixteen. God punished Korah and his followers by causing the ground to open and swallow them. In this Psalm we see that Korah's descendants, now the Korah family singers, are leading worship in church, good news for those who come from a dysfunctional family. Apparently, you can rise above your heritage.

Most likely, there was a circumstance that prompted the writing of this song. There is no way to know for sure, but it may have been when Absalom rebelled and took the kingdom from his father David. David not only was forced to flee but was betrayed by his own son. David probably wrote several psalms during that time.

All of us find ourselves in circumstances where our feelings test our faith. Maybe you've had times when you were in so much trouble that you were tempted to doubt God. Maybe you even felt guilty because of your doubt.

Is it appropriate to feel guilty because of feelings? Feelings aren't right or wrong. The ethical part of life is involved with our thoughts and actions. Feelings are involved with the emotional part of us. They aren't right or wrong…they just are.

Now we can categorize feelings into two groups. A feeling is based on either truth or a lie. This is important for us to realize because we have to learn to manage our feelings depending on which category they are in. Suppose you have a loved one who passes away. You experience the strongest emotions of your life. The emotions are based on truth, it has happened. What is the healthy way to deal with these emotions? You must grieve. In other words, in order to heal you must feel those emotions. It's not healthy to avoid them, deny them or to run from them. In order to heal you must face them. We don't ever suffer anything that Jesus hasn't also suffered, so the best place to bear these kinds of feelings is on his lap.

But then there are feelings that are based on lies. This happens often. We are constantly lied to.

Listen as Jesus speaks to some Jewish religious leaders:

> You belong to your father, the devil, and you want to carry out your father's desire. He was a murderer from the beginning, not holding to the truth, for there is no truth in him. When he lies, he speaks his native language, for he is a liar and the father of lies.

—John 8:44-45

So the father of lies whispers in your ear and tells you that you are ugly. You take that on and now you feel ugly. What do you do with emotions that are not based on truth? The healthy way to deal with those emotions is to speak the truth to them. "How can I be ugly when God says I am fearfully and wonderfully made?" Rather than dwell on lies, focus on the truth. Our emotions are a product of our thoughts, and so by speaking the truth to them, we slowly turn our emotions to the truth. That is what David is doing in this Psalm. This isn't a Psalm for those mornings where you wake up and say, "Good morning God." This is a Psalm for those times when you wake up and say, "Good God, it's morning!"

The Psalm traces three stages of the psalmist's experience with each stage ending with the refrain that describes what brought him through. The first stage describes an intense longing, along with the feeling that God is far away.

> As the deer pants for streams of water, so my soul pants for you, O God. My soul thirsts for God, for the living God. When can I go and meet with God?
>
> —Ps. 42:1-2

Picture a deer pursued by hunters on opening day of hunting season. The woods are full of hunters, and even though the deer is swift, it no sooner runs out of range of one hunter than it encounters a new threat. Eventually the deer becomes exhausted. It must keep running, but it is gasping for air and desperately in need of water.

To pant is to cry out in desperation. Have you ever been this desperate for God, this thirsty for his presence? Have you ever been low enough to be this frantic?

> My tears have been my food day and night, while men say to me all day long, "Where is your God?"

— Ps. 42:3

When you are in trouble and there is no God in sight, are you tempted to listen to the taunting enemy that whispers in your ear — "Where is your God?" The psalmist is determined that he will trust and hope in God. His emotions are screaming, "Where is God!" and yet his faith is strong.

> These things I remember as I pour out my soul: how I used to go with the multitude, leading the procession to the house of God, with shouts of joy and thanksgiving among the festive throng.

—Ps. 42:4

The psalmist is trying to build his confidence in God by remembering the good times. He is trying to bring his emotions in line with what he knows by faith to be the truth. You know, sometimes our human tendency is to only remember the bad things, "Oh yeah, that was the year the garage burned down." Some people keep a journal of blessings to help keep them riveted on the positive.

> Why are you downcast, O my soul? Why so disturbed within me? Put your hope in God, for I will yet praise him, my Savior and (my God).
>
> —Ps. 42:5

This is a great verse. God is a big God who loves you with a perfect love. He is on your side. You can trust him to always be there for you.

But the psalmist's trial is not over. He is still disheartened and so he goes on to stage two:

> My soul is downcast within me; therefore, I will remember you from the land of the Jordan, the heights of Hermon — from Mount Mizar. Deep calls to deep in the roar of your waterfalls; all your waves and breakers have swept over me. By day the LORD directs his love, at night his song is with me — a prayer to the God of my life.
>
> —Ps. 42:6-8

The Jordan River descends from north to south along the Jordan rift as it plummets from an elevation of 230 feet at Lake Huleh, finally emptying into the Sea of Galilee at 700 feet below sea level.

> ...it tears out on a run that, for some distance, brooks no restraint. It tumbles and cascades almost continuously through a forbidding, black basalt gorge. Foaming and muddy, it bursts out of the ravine. Then, collecting itself somewhat, it wriggles its way for about another mile through a small plain and a delta of its own making into the clear waters of the Lake of Galilee.
>
> —Nelson Glueck,
>
> The Jordan River, 35

David prays from the place of his exile, in the hills where the Jordan River cascades down. I picture him sitting beside a crashing waterfall. His mood matches his black basalt gorge environment as he desperately tries to collect his emotions and bring them in line with what he knows to be true. Verse seven reflects his emotions: "...all your waves and breakers have swept over me." Verse eight demonstrates his faith: "By day the LORD directs his love, at night his song is with me." It's important for us to learn to separate feelings from faith. Our feelings of doom in times of trouble don't mean that we aren't trusting God. Sometimes to trust is hanging on in spite of our feelings.

> I say to God my Rock, "Why have you forgotten me? Why must I go about mourning, oppressed by the enemy?" My bones suffer mortal agony as my foes taunt me, saying to me all day long, "Where is your God?"

—Ps. 42:9-10

David expresses his anguish over God's delay and the taunts of the enemy. Then to counter his feelings he again speaks the truth:

> Why are you downcast, O my soul? Why so disturbed within me? Put your hope in God, for I will yet praise him, my Savior and my God.

—Ps. 42:11

His agony continues as he finally despairs over his feelings that God has abandoned him. The danger is that those feelings, based on a lie, may become truth for David.

It is one thing for David to feel that God has abandoned him, another to believe it.

> Vindicate me, O God, and plead my cause against an ungodly nation; rescue me from deceitful and wicked men. You are God my stronghold. Why have you rejected me? Why must I go about mourning, oppressed by the enemy?
>
> —Ps. 43:1-2

David is tempted to begin believing his feelings. He is in trouble and he knows it. Next we have the key for times like this. Listen to the words of a man after God's own heart as he struggles to get on top of his depression.

> Send forth your light and your truth, let them guide me; let them bring me to your holy mountain, to the place where you dwell. Then will I go to the altar of God, to God, my joy and my delight. I will praise you with the harp, O God, my God. Why are you downcast, O my soul? Why so disturbed within me? Put your hope in God, for I will yet praise him, my Savior and my God.
>
> —Ps. 43:3-5

"Send forth your light and your truth." David asks for light and truth. He knows that God isn't defective but that his perception of God is. He knows that God loves him but that doesn't seem to line up with his circumstance; thus, he prays for light and truth. He is praying for God to speak, for a word from the Lord, for guidance from the God he trusts. "Your word is a lamp to my feet and a light for my path" (Ps 119:105).

I know! This is all easy to say when you are not going through a struggle. But what do you do when you are up to your ankles in the slimy pit (head first) and there seems no way out? When we are really miserable, how can we speak truth to our circumstances? It turns out that God has given us a formula to follow:

> ...for it is light that makes everything visible. This is why it is said: "Wake up, O sleeper, rise from the dead, and Christ will shine on you." Be very careful, then, how you live — not as unwise but as wise, making the most of every opportunity, because the days are evil. Therefore do not be foolish, but understand what the Lord's will is. Do

> not get drunk on wine, which leads to debauchery. Instead, be filled with the Spirit. Speak to one another with psalms, hymns and spiritual songs. Sing and make music in your heart to the Lord, always giving thanks to God the Father for everything, in the name of our Lord Jesus Christ.
>
> —Eph. 5:14-20

"Do not get drunk on wine." Many of us have been taught that living the Christian life is a matter of what not to fill ourselves with. In other words, if we will behave, then we will be acceptable to God. In times of distress and trouble we mostly feel guilty and unworthy of God's help. But verse eighteen uses wine merely to draw a contrast. The verse isn't about what not to fill ourselves with. We have somehow missed Paul's whole point. We think that by fulfilling the "no-no's" we will be holy. In this passage Paul is telling us that we are to be filled with the Holy Spirit. It's the presence of the Spirit that identifies us as the people of God. It's His Spirit that gives us strength and sustains us in times of struggle.

And so the formula for applying the truth to our feelings:

1. "Therefore do not be foolish, but understand what the Lord's will is."

2. "...be filled with the Spirit."

3. "Sing and make music in your heart to the Lord..."

4. "...always giving thanks to God the Father for everything, in the name of our Lord Jesus Christ."

Life Lesson

Knowing How God Lifts Us When We are Low

Consider and discuss: Think about the last time you felt despondent. What was the situation that caused those feelings?" Can you describe the feelings? Were the feelings based on truth or untruth?

Do you sometimes regard your down feelings as a lack of faith? Do you think there is a difference between faith and feelings? Can you have negative feelings and still have faith?

What do you do to turn your feelings around when you are depressed? Consider keeping a journal of blessings and referring to that journal during difficult times?

Read Eph. 5:14-20 again. Think about how you can use this formula to speak truth to your feelings.

Psalm 84

Hope for the Homeless

There are few stories that touch us as acutely as those of the homeless. We all know the sense of security and belonging that comes with having a home, a place where we can retreat for security, peace, and rest. Since spending time in India over the last decade, I've come to appreciate more than ever what it is to have a home. I've seen poor people who, having removed a sidewalk slab, dug a hole to make a home for their family of eight. I've seen single moms with three children living in a pup-tent-sized shelter made from palm branches and a blue plastic tarp. I sat on the shore of the Bay of Bengal after the 2004 tsunami and cried with a man over the rubble of what had been his house. These times have touched my heart as I imagine the uncertainty and anxiety of homelessness.

We all need a home, but a home is more than a place to hang your hat; it's also a place to belong. We all need a safe place that feels like home. "He who dwells in the shelter of the Most High will rest in the shadow of the Almighty. I will say of the Lord, 'He is my refuge and my fortress, my God, in whom I trust (Ps. 91:1-2)'. "

***

Psalm 84

This Psalm is for those who even though they may have a physical place to live are spiritually homeless. In Chris Tomlin's song, "I Will Rise," the lyrics perfectly express what it is to be at home with God:

> "There's a peace I've come to know
> Though my heart and flesh may fail
> There's an anchor for my soul
> I can say "It is well."

God intends to be the anchor for your soul. If you are not moored to God, if he is not at home in your heart, then it is not well with your soul. This Psalm teaches that even those who feel worthless and restless can find a home with their creator.

> How lovely is your dwelling place, O LORD Almighty! My soul yearns, even faints, for the courts of the LORD; my heart and my flesh cry out for the living God. Even the sparrow has found a home, and the swallow a nest for herself, where she may have her young — a place near your altar, O LORD Almighty, my King and my God. Blessed are those who dwell in your house; they are ever praising you. Selah
>
> —Ps. 84:1-4

By "your dwelling place" the author is referring to the temple. God's Shekinah glory was manifested in the temple. The Israelites could not enter physically into the Holy of Holies — where God dwelt — but the psalmist enters in spirit. He hadn't seen it and yet he appreciated the beauty of the place because he knew that God dwelt there.

Where is God's dwelling place today?

> Do you not know that your body is a temple of the Holy Spirit, who is in you, whom you have received from God? You are not your own;
>
> —1 Cor. 6:19

Read the verses again with joy, understanding that you are God's dwelling place:

> How lovely is your dwelling place, O LORD Almighty! My soul yearns, even faints, for the courts of the LORD; my heart and my flesh cry out for the living God. Even the sparrow has found a home, and the swallow a nest for herself, where she may have her young — a place near your altar, O LORD Almighty, my King and my God. Blessed are those who dwell in your house; they are ever praising you. Selah
>
> —Ps. 84:1-4

How lovely is his dwelling place? The heart where God lives becomes a beautiful place. The character of that heart is changed. When we grow in Christ we don't just get obedient, we get beautiful — lovely. And God's presence arouses in us a compelling hunger. "My soul yearns, even faints for the courts of the Lord." Haven't you ever longed for and craved more of the sense of His presence in your life? It is a strange paradox. God has the wonderful ability to satisfy us and at the same time make us hungry for more.

God's presence brings joyful energy into our lives. Our hearts and our flesh cry out for the living God. This, my friend, is what God meant for life to be like! If you don't have this joy, then you need to ask yourself who or what in your life has stolen the joy that God has given you. You may have been a Christian for years, but if you don't have this joy then you haven't touched the possibilities of the Christian life.

In light of all of this, do you see anything wrong with being bored? The woman at the well was bored. She had gone through five husbands and she was still bored. She had a live-in significant other and she was still bored. She drank from the well and she was thirsty again. Jesus' cure for her and us:

> But whoever drinks the water I give him will never thirst. Indeed, the water I give him will become in him a spring of water welling up to eternal life."
>
> —Jn. 4:14

How can we be bored with God living in us?

> Even the sparrow has found a home, and the swallow a nest for herself, where she may have her young — a place near your altar, O LORD Almighty, my King and my

God. Blessed are those who dwell in your house; they are ever praising you. Selah

—Ps. 84:3-4

The sparrow and the swallow are two common birds. Jesus used the sparrow to illustrate our value in God's eyes:

> Are not two sparrows sold for a penny? Yet not one of them will fall to the ground apart from the will of your Father. And even the very hairs of your head are all numbered. So don't be afraid; you are worth more than many sparrows.
>
> —Matt. 10:29-31

The sparrow is a symbol of insignificance. Sparrows represent those who feel valueless. The psalmist is expressing that even those who feel worthless find a home in God, a place of warmth and security, a refuge, a place of filling and contentment. There are many examples in the Bible where God has passed over the strong and powerful and used the obscure or insignificant to accomplish his purposes.

The swallow is the other bird mentioned. Swallows are swift birds that dart about, illustrating restless activity. Swallow-like people are those who are forever moving about, looking for something new. They go from thing to thing, job to job, place to place, relationship to relationship, church to church, looking for what will satisfy them. God offers a nest for swallows, a home for the restless.

> Come to me, all you who are weary and burdened, and I will give you rest. Take my yoke upon you and learn from me, for I am gentle and humble in heart, and you will find rest for your souls.
>
> —Matt. 11:28-29

These words are designed for living. God wants to give you rest. You won't find rest in leisure, adventure, or financial security.

> Blessed are those whose strength is in you, who have set their hearts on pilgrimage. As they pass through the Valley of Baca, they make it a place of springs; the autumn rains also cover it with pools. They go from strength to strength, till each appears before God in Zion. Hear my prayer, O LORD God Almighty; listen to me, O God of Jacob. Selah
>
> —Ps. 84:5-8

There is a great advantage in being in touch with the living God; he is where we find our strength. The words "who have set their hearts on pilgrimage" literally means, "In whose hearts are highways." What does that mean?

> A voice of one calling: "In the desert prepare the way for the LORD; make straight in the wilderness a highway for our God. Every valley shall be raised up, every mountain and hill made low; the rough ground shall become level, the rugged places a plain.
>
> —Isa. 40:3-4

This is work done in the heart. When you are in the low valleys of life, you are raised up through trust in God. When you are lifted high by the world, you judge yourself in the light of the Word of God and are brought low. You create in your heart a smooth highway for God to travel with blessings.

The Valley of Baca is a place in Israel named after a tree that is sticky on the outside because the sap weeps out. The Valley of Baca was an arid dry desert canyon that pilgrims would pass through on their way to Jerusalem to worship. It was known as the valley of weeping.

When you build highways in your heart for God to travel, when you give him access, you will go from the valley of weeping to a place of joy. You will go from strength to strength, getting better and better.

The psalmist is praying, "God, make me this kind of person. Help me build highways in my heart for you to travel so when I go through the valley of trials it will become a place of joy and I will get stronger and stronger until Jesus is seen in my life.

> Look upon our shield, O God; look with favor on your anointed one. Better is one day in your courts than a thousand elsewhere; I would rather be a doorkeeper in the house of my God than dwell in the tents of the wicked. For the LORD God is a sun and shield; the LORD bestows favor and honor; no good thing does he withhold from those whose walk is blameless. O LORD Almighty, blessed is the man who trusts in you.
>
> —Ps. 84:10-12

King David wrote this Psalm. This is a big statement coming from a man of royalty, wealth, and almost unlimited resources; to say that God is his shield, that he would rather spend a day in worship than a thousand doing anything else shows the heart of a man after God's own heart.

"For the LORD God is a sun and shield; the LORD bestows favor and honor; no good thing does he withhold from those whose walk is blameless." But wait, there is a condition for God's blessing. It seems he only gives unlimited goodness to "those whose walk is blameless." But who of us can be blameless?

> As it is written: "There is no one righteous, not even one; there is no one who understands, no one who seeks God. All have turned away, they have together become worthless; there is no one who does good, not even one." Now we know that whatever the law says, it says to those who are under the law, so that every mouth may be silenced and the whole world held accountable to God. Therefore, no one will be declared righteous in his sight by observing the law; rather, through the law we become conscious of sin.
>
> —Rom. 3:10-12, 19-20

No one will ever be good enough to be acceptable to God. He never intended it to work that way. He gave us his commandments, not as a list of rules to obey but rather to show us how impossible it would be for us to keep them. God has given his law and none of us has ever obeyed it completely. If we are judged according to God's law, we are all guilty. Fortunately for us, there is a "But now" in Romans 3:

> But now righteousness from God, apart from law, has been made known, to which the Law and the Prophets testify. This righteousness from God comes through faith in Jesus Christ to all who believe. There is no difference, for all have sinned and fall short of the glory of God, and are justified freely by his grace through the redemption that came by Christ Jesus. God presented him as a sacrifice of atonement, through faith in his blood. He did this to demonstrate his justice, because in his forbearance he had left the sins committed beforehand unpunished. He did it to demonstrate his justice at the present time, so as to be just and the one who justifies those who have faith in Jesus. Where then is boasting? It is excluded. On what

> principle? On that of observing the law? No, but on that of faith. For we maintain that a man is justified by faith apart from observing the law.
>
> —Rom. 3:21-28

God is a judge. It's part of his nature. He has to pour out his wrath on all unrighteousness. But God has given us a brand new way to be acceptable to him. He has given us a new righteousness to claim. He has satisfied his own nature by providing a substitute for our judgment. We have been judged and we are all guilty. There is no difference among us. We are all equally guilty and all deserve the same condemnation. But because of his love for us, the father has placed all of our punishment and condemnation on his own son. He sacrificed his son to save us. "For all have sinned and fall short of the glory of God." This verse reveals God's intention for us. It's not his glory that we fall short of but the glory he has planned for us. We are to be on display for all eternity as God's best creative effort. Our lives are to reflect his glory.

"O LORD Almighty, blessed is the man who trusts in you" (Ps. 84:12). Are you blessed? Blessing is what happens when you make contact with the living God. The word blessed literally means, "to be level." When the storms of life rage, then a level person is lifted up above the storm (blessed) because he trusts in God.

God is reaching for all those who have drifted away. He wants to renew his relationship and bless all those who have gone their own way. If you have drifted away I have a message for you. God called...he wants you back. He wants you to make your home in him.

Life Lesson

Finding a Home in God

Consider and discuss: Home is a place where we feel secure. Has your home ever been burglarized or vandalized? Describe how you felt when you discovered that your property had been violated.

This Psalm teaches us that we can have a spiritual home with God. Describe what that means to you.

Have you ever had feelings of worthlessness? Describe how you felt about yourself. How has this Psalm helped you to see your true value?

Restless people are those who are forever moving about, looking for something new. They go from thing to thing, job to job, place to place, relationship to relationship, church to church, looking for what will satisfy them. Does this describe you? Why?

What does it mean to you that you are to build highways in your heart for God to travel?

Psalm 91

Hope for the Vulnerable

I contracted polio during the Polio Epidemic of 1946. Both my arms and legs were paralyzed as well as my diaphragm. The doctors told my parents that I would not survive. At the time there was a Catholic nun, Sister Kenney, who had developed an experimental program to treat this dreaded disease; thus, my parents brought me to her clinic. I was wrapped in hot towels to drive out the infection. The treatment saved my life but I was left with a paralyzed left arm. As I grew, I became self-conscious of my withered and atrophied muscles. When I became a Christian, I began to question God about my infirmity. Why would he heal me through Sister Kenney, but not completely? Many had prayed for me. Why didn't God restore my arm? Over time, God has not healed my arm but he has healed my spirit. His words to the Apostle Paul ring in my heart. "My grace is sufficient for you, for my power is made perfect in [your] weakness" (2 Cor 12:9). I sometimes wonder who I would have become if I hadn't had polio. In his wisdom, did the Lord give me a great gift that I won't truly appreciate until I stand in his presence?

I submit to you that God's love and power is sufficient to bring us through anything, and then on to glory. That's how we get through life. It's okay to be afraid; we are his children. There is much we don't understand but we hold his hand tightly as we walk at his side.

Maybe you were thinking you might skip this Psalm because you don't see yourself as particularly vulnerable. Many people don't like to think of themselves as weak; but if you are considering giving this Psalm a pass, I'd advise against it. The book of Job teaches us that even those who are the best and strongest among us are vulnerable: "Yet man is born to trouble as surely as sparks fly upward" (Job 5:7).

Let's face it, Job was right; it's as sure as gravity. We will have trouble in this world and we're not going to get through it without problems. Some have come to the mistaken conclusion that they have made God angry and are just getting what they deserve. But the point of this Psalm is that when we go through difficult times, God will help us if we abide in Him.

God's promise in this Psalm is that when we find ourselves in need, he will be with us and will bring us through it. God may keep you from trouble, but if he does not, <u>he promises to be with you in it</u>. We won't always know why he does one or the other.

The original setting of the Psalm is unknown. We don't even know the author. It could have been King David or possibly Moses. One thing we do know is that the psalmist is describing the on-going sovereign protection of God's people; that God is ever protecting them in all the dangers and terrors that surround them. Literally, the Psalm will be fulfilled in the Messianic kingdom, and we see that it depicts prophetically what will happen on the earth in that future time when the lion will lie down with the lamb. But in a very real and concrete way, this Psalm speaks to us today. No matter what circumstance you find yourself in, God is saying, "I will protect you; I will be with you."

***

Psalm 91

There are two things we have to be certain of before we will be willing to hope in God for our protection. Is he both able and willing to be our protector? The psalmist answers these questions by giving us some names of God that reveal his character:

> He who dwells in the shelter of the Most High will rest in the shadow of the Almighty.
>
> —Ps. 91:1

The first name we are given is "Most High." It's the Hebrew word, "Elyon," which means, "the one who owns and is above everything." God is your creator and you belong to him. Second, we see the name "Almighty," "El-Shaddai," which means "mighty in grace." He is El-Shaddai — the almighty God of grace. You can trust him; he is both willing and able to help you.

God wants us to rest in him, not the things of the world. Dare we even go there? Many of us live as though we belong to this world and to this present age, but we do not. We are in the world, but we belong to the age to come. And yet many of us put roots down deep into our fallen culture and act as though this is where we belong. I suspect that you are where I am on this one. I love to talk about how I am not of this world but of a heavenly kingdom; and yet that attitude changes when they come for my stuff. God says: "Come out from among them and be separate. I will be a father to you and you will be my sons and daughters. I will take care of you. I am God Almighty, El-Shaddai." The psalmist is telling us that he is a God in whom you can hope. You can trust in his character. When times turn sour he is the God you can turn to for help.

> He who dwells in the shelter of the Most High will rest in the shadow of the Almighty.
>
> —Ps. 91:1

You can rest in his shadow. Remember that Israel is a land of great heat. The sun bore down on the people day after day as they worked in the fields. Barb and I lived a few years in the Southwest Arizona desert; we know that oppressive heat well. I can remember many hikes in the desert where even a small bush would provide a welcome relief from the blazing sun. Resting in the shadow of the almighty is a metaphor for the care and protection of God:

He is shade in the midst of the scorching heat of this cruel world.

> I will say of the Lord, "He is my refuge and my fortress, my God, in whom I trust."
>
> —Ps. 91:2

He is God "Most High," he is "God Almighty," and now he is "LORD." The name Lord is Yahweh, the covenant-keeping God. He is the unchangeable "I Am." Ever notice that when trouble comes your friends sort of thin out. Your friends may back off when things turn on you, but Jesus loves to come to your rescue. When the going is hard, he'll be there. He is the Most High and he will lift you up. He is El-Shaddai, the Almighty God of Grace who will meet your needs and lift you out of the slimy pit. He is the LORD, Yahweh, the covenant-keeping God, who will never leave you.

When God is your friend he will never abandon you.

> Surely he will save you from the fowler's snare and from the deadly pestilence.
>
> —Ps. 91:3

He protects us from the fowler's snare, a picture of birds caught in a trap. Yes, there is a devil and he does set traps to catch us. Jesus also saves us from pestilence, the evil that comes to us because we live in a fallen world. If you are abiding in God, he will defend you from both.

> He will cover you with his feathers, and under his wings you will find refuge; his faithfulness will be your shield and rampart.
>
> —Ps. 91:4

This is a picture of a mama bird wooing her chicks and tucking them safely underneath her wings. We can take refuge in the shadow of his wings until danger has passed. It seems so removed from how we think about Almighty God. But he refers to himself as a mother hen, always watching over her brood, always willing to take them under her wings to guard them, and to even die for them if necessary.

I think about the woman in the Bible who was caught in adultery? If you asked for her testimony she would say: "They were after me. They condemned me and they were going to stone me. But I was brought before Jesus, and in tenderness he became my protector and he said to me, 'I don't condemn you, your sins are forgiven, go in peace.'" Jesus wants to be our shield from those who would accuse and condemn us. He tells us what he told that woman: "Where are those who condemn you? I have sent them away. I don't condemn you. You are forgiven. Go in peace and sin no more."

"His faithfulness will be your shield and rampart." The shield and rampart are for defense. We know what a shield is; it's for warding off the blows of the enemy. A rampart is a wall; it's a covering that goes around you that keeps the enemy from getting to you. His faithfulness is both shield and rampart. Many Christians today are confused about how to react to struggles. Are we to just battle through as best we can; or is it more spiritual to deny our problems all together? After all, doesn't God want us to be healthy and worry free? Should we just put on a happy face and believe that God will lift us out of our problems? I suggest to you that it is neither.

We are children of the King of Kings, royal children of the supreme being of the universe. To think that we are dumped on this earth to just fight on our own would be the unthinkable act of an unloving parent. But neither is it valid to think that we have a right to expect God to just lift us out of our difficulties. There is a belief that says that if you have faith you will be rich, healthy, happy, and trouble free, and that if you don't have these things there is something spiritually wrong with you. But God never promises that you will be rich and struggle free. Maybe it's that you have sinned and he is punishing you. Or perhaps there is something wrong with God, that he is either unwilling or unable to pull you out of this mess. I suggest to you that it is none of the above.

In his book, "The Prisoner in the Third Cell," author Gene Edwards, tells the story of John the Baptist. John has been imprisoned by King Herod and is on death row awaiting his execution. But he is Jesus' cousin; surely Jesus will save him. John reasons to himself in his prison cell; "he is the Messiah — isn't he?" John's life is on the line; he has to know for sure. He sends two of his disciples to go find Jesus and ask him if in fact he is the Messiah.

After some time John's disciples return. "Well, what did you find out? Is he indeed the Messiah? Did you ask him?" "Yes," they replied. "We asked him." "What did he say?" "He said, 'Go and tell John that the sick are healed, the lame walk, the blind see and the deaf hear.'" John asks, "Is it true? Did Jesus heal people?" "Yes," they replied. "We saw healings with our own eyes." Excitedly, John asked, "Everyone that came to him was healed?" "No," they said, "Not everyone. Some came to him but he did not heal them." John pondered this for a long time and then asked, "Did he say anything else?" "Yes," they said. "He said, 'Blessed is he who is not offended by me.'"

This story has had a profound impact on my theology of healing. Not everyone is healed. Not everyone is lifted out of their crisis. "Blessed is he who is not offended by me." Now I want to be very clear. I'm not saying that God will not deliver you out of your struggles. He may very well do just that. He is a sovereign, omnipotent God who can do anything, and he loves you. He is a healing God and a God who loves to give good gifts to his children. God can and often does deliver his children from pain, sickness, and trials.

But sometimes he doesn't...and it's that "sometimes" that is the cause of so much confusion and misunderstanding among Christians. Many times we join the psalmist in Psalm 42 when he cries out, "Where is [my] God?" We are in a brawl with the enemy and there is no God to come to the rescue. Isn't that sometimes your experience? Where is your God? Many people who come to God and seek deliverance or healing are never delivered, never healed.

So what do we do? Is this whole Christianity thing a farce? You have God, who says he will cover you with his feathers and be your refuge; all the while, you sit there sick, a lost job, a pile of bills you can't pay, and relationships in the dumpster. Where is God?

The answer is to discover the presence of God in the middle of your circumstance. Knowing that God is with you will make all the difference.

If you discover the presence of God, then even though you go through distress, the distress won't go through you.

God is too big and his motives are too high for us to ever understand him, but we must know that he is for us. If we dwell in the secret place of the Most High, and if we focus on the great character of God, and make him our dwelling place, we can know that we are protected. How wonderful if he lifts us out of our suffering. But there is an even greater deliverance, one where he walks with us in our fight rather than rescuing us from it. Together with Jesus, we can walk through a nightmare without fear.

We may pass through the deep water but it cannot flow over us. We may walk through the fire but will not be burned. If we go through hell, it cannot touch us because the king is at our side.

> You will not fear the terror of night, nor the arrow that flies by day, nor the pestilence that stalks in the darkness, nor the plague that destroys at midday.
>
> —Ps. 91:5-6

It's okay to be afraid, but as you walk at his side you will learn that there is nothing to fear. You have God's hand; therefore, there is no terror that can harm you.

Look at the first six words of verse five: "You will not fear the terror." Okay, hit the pause button. That is a totally illogical phrase. It's not only illogical, it is unnatural. How can you not fear it if it is a terror? Let me give you an example — you are downtown walking on the sidewalk and you decide to cross the street. Absent-mindedly you step off the sidewalk into the street. You turn your head only to see a very large bus heading straight for you. Instantly terror strikes your heart and the natural fear of that terror causes you to jump very quickly back onto the sidewalk.

Or what if your problem is finances? You cannot pay your bills and terror wells up in your heart, but there is nowhere to jump. That is the situation many of us find ourselves in these days. We are wracked with fear, anxiety, and worry over an unknown future.

The wonderful, illogical, unnatural thing the psalmist is saying here is that you will not fear the terror because God has you by the hand and he will not let go. He smiles at you and says — "Walk with me and fear not." How cool to walk the path of danger with the God of the universe at your side and his arm around you.

> But now, this is what the Lord says — he who created you, he who formed you, "Fear not, for I have redeemed you; I have summoned you by name; you are mine. When you pass through the waters, I will be with you; and when you pass through the rivers, they will not sweep over you. When you walk through the fire, you will not be burned; the flames will not set you

ablaze. For I am the Lord, your God, the Holy One of Israel, your Savior.

—Isa. 43:1-3

God doesn't promise that you won't go through the water; he doesn't say that you won't go through the fire. He says the water won't drown you and the fire won't burn you. That is rejoicing in the madness of the storm; it's dancing in the downpour. How good is that! To the world it is absolutely crazy and foolish — "but the foolishness of God is wiser than the wisdom of men." Do you get it? It's not about being delivered out of your crises; it's about him delivering you right in the middle of them.

Think about Daniel in that lion's den. God didn't send lightning down to burn up the lions; although, he certainly could have. He didn't open a trap door in the bottom of the den and cause them to drop out. No, he didn't remove the lions at all. He just shut their mouths.

Consider the three men in the fiery furnace. God could have reached down and delivered them a second before they went in the furnace, but he didn't. These three men had to go through the fire. But Jehovah made it so that the fire had no power to burn them, and in fact, he was right there with them in the fire. How fun!

Do you get it? To go through something terrible and not be afraid because you are dwelling under the wing of Almighty God — to stand up straight and stare down that giant blocking your path — that is how you get through this life. The Lord wants us to walk in joy and confidence, knowing that we are children of the living King.

Now the psalmist outlines some specific things that we may go through:

> You will not fear the terror of night, nor the arrow that flies by day, nor the pestilence that stalks in the darkness, nor the plague that destroys at midday.
>
> —Ps. 91:5-6

The psalmist gives us two kinds of terror to not fear. There is the kind that comes at night and the kind that comes in the day. There is the terror that comes in the dark and the kind that comes in the light.

Those things that come by night are the battles you don't see coming. One day you are fine and the next you are in the emergency room. Or you thought everything was fine in your family and now suddenly you are thrust in the middle of a crisis.

Then there are terrors that come by day; you see them coming but you are powerless to stop them. You've watched your savings slip away; you are powerless to change things.

The psalmist says you will not fear any of these things because you dwell in the shadow of the Almighty; he's got your back. This is awesome; this is the hope that a believer can have. Why? Because God is so great that he's not just able to lift you out of life's skirmishes, he is able to give you victory right in the middle of them.

> A thousand may fall at your side, ten thousand at your right hand, but it will not come near you.
>
> —Ps. 91:7

Hey, they may be dropping like flies all around you, but this thing will not touch you because the everlasting wings protect you. Instead of running to God when you are in trouble, if you will run to God every day, abide in him, and dwell in his presence, then it doesn't matter even if something comes on you suddenly because he already has your hand.

> You will only observe with your eyes and see the punishment of the wicked. If you make the Most High your dwelling — even the Lord, who is my refuge — then no harm, will befall you, no disaster will come near your tent.
>
> —Ps. 91:8-10

Sometimes God allows us to go through the smelting furnace, the refiner's fire; his purpose is not to burn us, but to burn off the dross, the impurities that keep us from enjoying eternity with him. God has the big picture. Let's learn to cooperate with him and trust him in the storm as we nestle under his wing.

This is how the Christian stands firm. Everything around you may go to pieces, but you won't.

Will you trust Him? I'm not saying you won't bleed; I'm not saying you won't be heartbroken or experience pain. God isn't saying grit your teeth and bear it. He's saying, "Put your hope in me; I will see you through it and make it all work out for your good."

***

How can I know for sure? Are there any assurances of God's help?

> If you make the Most High your dwelling — even the Lord, who is my refuge — then no harm will befall you, no disaster will come near your tent. For he will command his angels concerning you to guard you in all your ways; they will lift you up in their hands, so that you will not strike your foot against a stone.
>
> —Ps. 91:9-12

The first thing we should notice in this passage is that God's help is not unconditional. The passage says that if we make the Most High our dwelling, then we are assured of his protection.

How does he protect us? "For he will command his angels concerning you…" The Lord assigns these great celestial beings to guard us. We have superheroes sent to be with us, support us, guard us, and protect us? From the day that you took your first breath, the command went out from the throne room of God — "Send my trusted companions to be with him. Stay with her all her life. Guard him; support her through to salvation and beyond."

This passage about angels is so significant that even the devil has memorized it and used it to tempt Jesus. Let's go to that showdown moment in the desert. In this scene we have the prince of fallen angels and the King of Angels as they meet together on the hot desert sand of the wilderness temptation:

> Then Jesus was led by the Spirit into the desert to be tempted by the devil. After fasting forty days and forty nights, he was hungry. The tempter came to him and said, "If you are the Son of God, tell these stones to become bread." Jesus answered, "It is written: 'Man does not live on bread alone, but on every word that comes from the mouth of God.'"

> Then the devil took him to the holy city and had him stand on the highest point of the temple. "If you are the Son of God," he said, "throw yourself down. For it is written: "'He will command his angels concerning you, and they will lift you up in their hands, so that you will not strike your foot against a stone.'"
>
> —Matt. 4:1-6

Satan tempts him on the pinnacle of the temple — "Jump Jesus! The angels will catch you." Satan quotes Psalm 91, but he intentionally omits a line he doesn't want Jesus, or us, to hear: "For he will command his angels concerning you *to guard you in all your ways*" (Ps. 91:11 italics mine).

The tempter didn't want to remind Jesus that the angels were always with him to guard him in all his ways, and he doesn't want us to know either.

Now don't get obsessed with angels; they are our guardians, powerful beings, and God's protection! If your emphasis is on the angels, you're missing the whole point. Look beyond the angels to recognize that Christ has ordained them to guard us. They are not our focus but his protection. We don't need to see angels, we need to see Jesus! We don't talk to angels, we talk to Jesus.

***

Most of us have learned to be skeptics. Our bias is to distrust people, often with good reason. There's a fair chance that as you read this there is someone trying to steal your stuff, your good name, or your identity. I didn't just get off the turnip truck. I know that I can't believe everything I hear, read, or every promise made. That's a good thing...or is it? Could it be that I am now so conditioned to have a bias for being wary that I have a hard time trusting the one person in this universe that I can trust unconditionally? Is God too good to be true?

Christian trust is outrageous. We are asked to put our faith and trust in God, who we cannot hear or see, to trust him with big things and small, with our very lives. Can he really be trusted?

Do we believe that He is a God of his word; that he will come through for us? Do we believe that his grace is sufficient for our need; that he will go through the water with us? Do we believe that he will keep the fire from burning us? When we go through the valley of the shadow of death, do we believe that he will be with us? Do we believe that his rod and staff will comfort us?

Do we really believe it? At the end of this Psalm God gives us six promises. Can we receive them? Can we believe him for them? Sometimes we have to eat our words, but God will never eat his. God himself is the assurance of his own words. He stands behind what he says. Is God limited by anything? Yes! God limits himself by his own promises. He limits himself to his word because when God declares something, it is finished.

If this is true, and it is, then what greater rebellion, what greater insult to God can there be than to not believe his promises. Someone said, "It is better to be going through hell with a promise than to live in paradise without one." God's promises mean everything.

So at the end of the Psalm God gives us six promises:

> "Because he loves me," says the Lord, "I will rescue him; I will protect him, for he acknowledges my name. He will call upon me, and I will answer him; I will be with him in trouble, I will deliver him and honor him. With long life will I satisfy him and show him my salvation."
>
> —Ps. 91:14-16

First, God promises to rescue us. It is cause and effect. He says, "Because he loves me; therefore, I will rescue him." What does God do when he delivers us? Think about it. God steps out of eternity into time; he steps into our world to intervene. But there is a condition, and the condition is that you love him. It's not carte blanche for every person. God reserves his rescue for those who love him. "And we know that in all things God works for the good of those who love him, who have been called according to his purpose" (Rom. 8:28). There is no assurance outside of Christ; he is the way, the truth, and the life. You need Christ! You need to fall in love with him. Love will drive you to God; and if you're driven to him, you'll be protected by him.

How do I love God like that? How do I make that work? Let's get practical. Go back for a second to verse 9: "If you make the Most High your dwelling." It's the word "dwelling." It literally means "habitation." It's the place where you live. Make Elyon — the Most High your habitation, your home. Move in with Jesus. Spend time with him, include him in everything you do, and see if you fall in love.

God's second promise is, "I will protect him, for he acknowledges my name." This is a great promise. It means that God will lift you above your circumstances. It's a promise. I remember reading about what eagles do when they're soaring in the sky and the crows come and pester them in mid-flight by pecking on their wings. The eagles soar higher to an altitude that the crows cannot reach. That is what God does for us when we dwell underneath His wing; he lifts us above our struggles.

It may take faith to believe for a miracle, but it takes more faith to trust God when the miracles don't come. Sometimes we need to have the faith of Job when he said, "Though he slay me, yet will I trust Him."

The third promise is, "He will call upon me, and I will answer him."

> Before they call I will answer; while they are still speaking I will hear.
>
> —Isa. 65:24

It's a promise. Even before we cry out, he answers.

The fourth promise is, "I will be with him in trouble." He will be with us. You know how calming it is when you are going through a great struggle to have someone who will just be with you, hold your hand and hang with you. If you've ever been with someone in a great time of need, you know there is little you can do to help; just your presence strengthens them. But here we have the God of the universe promising to be with us in our struggle, and he is not helpless. He can change things.

The fifth promise is, "I will deliver him and honor him."

> Jesus said: "Whoever serves me must follow me; and where I am, my servant

also will be. My Father will honor the one who serves me."

—John 12:26

God hasn't promised us an easy time, but one thing he has promised — a safe arrival to Glory; he'll get us there. When we see his face we shall be like him. That work he began in us and continues in us, he will bring to completion. If you believe that, what is there to fear? God is a God of his word, and the resurrection is our ultimate assurance.

Sixthly, and finally, he promises, "With long life will I satisfy him and show him my salvation."

I read this Psalm to my dad on his deathbed. When I got to this verse it made me pause in my spirit. My dad's days were over; he was dying young. What could Jesus possibly be saying? But the words are true. My dad came to know Jesus several years before his death. He had experienced salvation and now would be living with his savior for eternity.

If you know Jesus he promises personal fulfilment, satisfaction, and enjoyment of salvation. You'd think a person couldn't enjoy salvation to look at me some days. If you have Jesus in your life, then you have received the greatest gift ever given. Enjoy it! God intends that you live your life in victory and fulfilment. In fact, he promises it. Receive it!

Whatever circumstance you find yourself in today, flee to the hope that is Christ. Let him be your anchor in the midst of the storm. If you dwell in him, love him, and call upon him today, then all of Psalm 91 is yours. What a treasure.

Life Lesson

Knowing God's Protection

Consider and discuss: Do you have it settled in your heart that God is both willing and able to protect you? Explain.

> He will cover you with his feathers, and under his wings you will find refuge; his faithfulness will be your shield and rampart.

—Ps. 91:4

How does the above verse make you feel? Describe what it is to be covered by his wings.

What do you do when you need God's protection and you call out to him but he doesn't answer? Can you relate a time when this happened? How did you respond?

Have you ever been through a difficult time but you were filled with faith and felt God's sustaining presence. Try to remember and share the details of that experience.

Psalm 107

Hope for the Unloved

My son Dave is the best fisherman I know. He usually catches more fish than anyone else, and it isn't luck. He is driven, determined, and intentional about his technique and his tackle. He never stays in one spot long but continues on to the next bay or patch of weeds, always looking for the elusive prey. He catches more fish because he works harder, pursues it with a relentless passion, and never gives up.

Dave's tenacity is a picture of God's love for us. God pursues us with a ceaseless passion. Before you were saved you were like Adam, lost to God, separated from him by your sin. After Adam sinned, God walked in the garden crying "Adam, where are you?" I believe that God was literally weeping. As a Christian, it's unbelief or a lack of faith that causes a separation between you and God. He's still searching, seeking, and pursuing us, but our doubt comes between us and God. He never stops seeking, never stops crying out "Adam, where are you?" God's love is infinite; he will never stop loving you. If you feel unloved today then this psalm is for you.

***

Psalm 107

How do we respond to a God of endless love?

> Give thanks to the LORD, for he is good; his love endures forever.
>
> —Ps. 107:1

God's love is his pure unqualified acceptance. God accepts us just the way we are. We don't have to live up to some standard. We don't earn his love. God's character is to love. He accepts us as we are and then he sets out to make us into what we are longing to be. God made each of us as a specific individual with a specific place and role in his kingdom. We will never be satisfied and fulfilled unless we become the person he made us to be. Deep inside each of us is longing to be that person.

> Let the redeemed of the LORD say this — those he redeemed from the hand of the foe, those he gathered from the lands, from east and west, from north and south.
>
> —Ps. 107:2-3

"Let the redeemed of the LORD say this..." Say what? "Give thanks to the LORD, for he is good; his love endures forever." Let's never forget to thank him for his love for us. It is a gift we will never deserve and without it we would be doomed. Giving thanks to the Lord is how we love him back. The Bible is filled with instruction on giving thanks. You will find the phrase, "give thanks to the Lord," and, "his love endures forever," over and over in the Bible.

Who are the redeemed? What does it mean to be redeemed? The Hebrew word translated "redeemed" means "to make kin." In the Bible, to redeem someone means that you bring them into your family. The custom in Bible times was that if a man died, his brother would marry his widow. Actually, any member of a man's family could marry his widow to take care of her. The man would be known as a kinsman-redeemer. The widow would become his wife and her children would become his children. God redeemed us from sin that same way. Jesus is our kinsman-redeemer.

Think for a moment what it means to forgive an enemy? For us, the best we can do in forgiving is to no longer hold it against someone for how they've wronged us. But God doesn't just forgive — he redeems, he makes us his bride and his children. "Give thanks to the LORD, for he is good; his love endures forever."

There is a story in the Bible of a time when Jesus was invited to dinner at a religious leader's home. As Jesus reclined at the table he was approached by a woman who had a poor reputation, having led a sinful life. The woman had an alabaster jar of perfume and she knelt before Jesus and wept as her tears fell on his feet. The woman then dried Jesus' feet with her hair, kissed them, and poured the expensive perfume on his feet. When the host of the dinner saw this, he turned to his other guests and said, "If this man was really a prophet, he would have known what kind of a woman she is and wouldn't have anything to do with her." Jesus turned to the host and said:

> "Simon, I have something to tell you." "Tell me, teacher," he said. "Two men owed money to a certain moneylender. One owed him five hundred denarii, and the other fifty. Neither of them had the money to pay him back, so he canceled the debts of both. Now which of them will love him more?" Simon replied, "I suppose the one who had the bigger debt canceled." "You have judged correctly," Jesus said. Then he turned toward the woman and said to Simon, "Do you see this woman? I came into your house. You did not give me any water for my feet, but she wet my feet with her tears and wiped them with her hair. You did not give me a kiss, but this woman from the time I entered, has not stopped kissing my feet. You did not put oil on my head, but she has poured perfume on my feet. Therefore, I tell you, her many sins have been forgiven — for she loved much. But he who has been forgiven little, loves little." Then Jesus said to her, "Your sins are forgiven." The other guests began to say among themselves, "Who is this who even forgives sins?" Jesus said to the

> woman, "Your faith has saved you; go in peace."
>
> —Luke 7:40-50

Jesus turned to the woman and told her that her sins were forgiven. What prompted him to do that? There is no indication that he forgave the sins of the others present. The difference was that she grieved over her sin. She cried out for forgiveness while the others were too self-righteous to even recognize their need for forgiveness. God isn't slow to forgive; he is actively seeking those who will receive his forgiveness. He is in the business of redeeming and gathering his children.

Read these words of Jesus and catch a glimpse of the heart of God:

> O Jerusalem, Jerusalem, you who kill the prophets and stone those sent to you, how often I have longed to gather your children together, as a hen gathers her chicks under her wings, but you were not willing.
>
> —Matt. 23:37

Jesus wept as he said those words.

***

In the next section of the Psalm, the psalmist describes how God demonstrates his loving acceptance of us and how he reaches out and finds us when we cry to him. It is given to us in the form of four testimonies. Think about these testimonies. You may spot yourself in one of them.

Testimony #1 - Restless people:

> Some wandered in desert wastelands, finding no way to a city where they could settle. They were hungry and thirsty, and their lives ebbed away. Then they cried out to the LORD in their trouble, and he delivered them from their distress.
>
> —Ps. 107:4-6

I understand the desert wasteland. I know what it is for lips to be dry and cracked as you wander looking for water. Some people live their lives that way. With unfulfilled hunger and thirst, they wander from thing to thing in their lives, but no matter what they try nothing satisfies them. Lives ebb away. Waves come on strong from the ocean and they crash with power against the shore, but then they dribble back weakly having expended all their energy. Some people are like this. They have big plans and dreams and are solid for a time, but lose hope and sink back.

Who are these people and what are they looking for? There are people today who wander in desert wastelands looking for a place to settle? We could call them, "the restless ones." They are trying to fill a gap in their lives. They wander from place to place, job to job, church to church, or relationship to relationship. These are people who feel an ache within and they desperately search to fill the void. Their lives seem empty.

"Some wandered in desert wastelands, finding no way to a city where they could settle." The psalmist says that they are looking for a city. A city gives us the advantage of excitement and security. There is an excitement wherever people gather together; it's where the action is. Excitement is something we need. There is nothing worse than being lonely and bored. Some of the restless ones today are seeking excitement at the price of their health or even their lives. They seek a false excitement that can only lead to despair. But God never intended life to be boring.

Walking with him is the greatest adventure we can imagine.

A city is also a place of security, a place where we can rest, where we can find a home. These restless ones can't find a city like that. They are "hungry and thirsty, and their lives ebb away." In Bible days, people lived together in cities for protection. It doesn't quite work that way today.

Are you one of these wanderers — hungry and thirsty for life but never finding it? Maybe you know of the abundant life in Christ but can't make it happen for you. You live as a Christian — at least you go through all the motions — but you are never truly satisfied. You don't know where to turn or how to change. The testimony of this Psalm is your answer!

> Then they cried out to the LORD in their trouble, and he delivered them from their distress. He led them by a straight way to a city where they could settle.
>
> —Ps. 107:6-7

They cried out to the Lord. Just like the sinful woman at Simon's home. God finds those who cry out to him, those who are wandering in circles, and he shows them a straight way. What did these criers do to tap into the love of God? How did they qualify for his loving acceptance?

God is never far away; in fact, he's searching for you. God is the lover of lovers. He never stops seeking, never stops searching. The only step of faith he needs in order to pluck you out of your troubles and deliver you from your distress is for you to cry out to him.

He shows us a straight way to a city, a place of adventure and security, a place where life is full and all of it wrapped in the arms of God. God finds those who are lost in their confusion and wanderings and cry out to him. He gathers us as an anxious groom gathers his bride, as a hen gathers her children, and he gives us a home so we will no longer wander.

Aren't you glad that you don't have to qualify for his love? God is as close as he can be, just waiting for us to reach for him.

> He said to me: "It is done. I am the Alpha and the Omega, the Beginning and the End. To him who is thirsty I will give to

> drink without cost from the spring of the water of life.
>
> —Rev. 21:6

The Lord loves to find those who are lost and wandering and give them a home. How do we respond to this great love?

> Let them give thanks to the LORD for his unfailing love and his wonderful deeds for men, for he satisfies the thirsty and fills the hungry with good things.
>
> —Ps. 107:8-9

***

Testimony #2 - Crushed people:

> Some sat in darkness and the deepest gloom, prisoners suffering in iron chains, for they had rebelled against the words of God and despised the counsel of the Most High. So he subjected them to bitter labor; they stumbled, and there was no one to help.
>
> —Ps. 107:10-12

This is a picture of someone who knows God, but is unable to accept his love or see that he is in control. This is a picture of a person who fails to put God first but relies on someone or something else for his security. "Some sat in darkness and the deepest gloom." When that thing that we have put our confidence in, that thing that defines our self-image, lets us down, then depression will follow as the tent poles are pulled out.

"Prisoners suffering in iron chains…" This is a description of a person in bondage, a slave to a false perception. This person feels worthless, ugly, or that their life doesn't count.

"They had rebelled against the words of God and despised the counsel of the Most High." These aren't bad people. They rebelled against God because they have a poor picture of who he is. They can't see how much he loves them.

"So he subjected them to bitter labor; they stumbled, and there was no one to help." It sounds exactly like a job I had once.

But there is good news. There is a power that can cut through the dark gloom and break the iron chains.

> Then they cried to the LORD in their trouble, and he saved them from their

> distress. He brought them out of darkness and the deepest gloom and broke away their chains. Let them give thanks to the LORD for his unfailing love and his wonderful deeds for men, for he breaks down gates of bronze and cuts through bars of iron.
>
> —Ps. 107:13-16

***

Testimony # 3 - Blind people:

> Some became fools through their rebellious ways and suffered affliction because of their iniquities. They loathed all food and drew near the gates of death.
>
> —Ps. 107:17-18

No one likes to be called a fool. This is a person who is suffering and unable to receive wisdom because he has rebelled against the love of God in his life. These are people who are suffering from false perceptions of who they are. They are people who are fearful, nervous, and afraid to face life. They are sure that God is mad at them. In their inability to accept God's love they have wrapped themselves up so tight within themselves that they are unable to love or be loved; it is eating them up. They cannot find peace.

There is an answer for these people as well when they cry out to the living God.

> Then they cried to the LORD in their trouble, and he saved them from their distress. He sent forth his word and healed them; he rescued them from the grave. Let them give thanks to the LORD for his unfailing love and his wonderful deeds for men. Let them sacrifice thank offerings and tell of his works with songs of joy.
>
> —Ps. 107:19-22

"He sent forth his word and healed them." I love that. I wonder what verses he sent them. Maybe he sent them John 8:32: "Then you will know the truth, and the truth will set you free."

***

Testimony #4 - Fearful people:

These are those who have put their confidence in something other than God, and when that thing lets them down, they are caught up in fear:

> Others went out on the sea in ships; they were merchants on the mighty waters. They saw the works of the LORD, his wonderful deeds in the deep. For he spoke and stirred up a tempest that lifted high the waves. They mounted up to the heavens and went down to the depths; in their peril their courage melted away. They reeled and staggered like drunken men; they were at their wits' end.
>
> —Ps. 107:23-27

The scriptures often use the sea as a picture of life. This is the testimony of people who are rocked by circumstances. They are paralyzed with fear and at their wits end.

Many have put their confidence in their career. Then things happen — layoffs, unemployment, a nasty boss, mean customers, a poor economy, financial problems, and so on, ad infinitum.

> Then they cried out to the LORD in their trouble, and he brought them out of their distress. He stilled the storm to a whisper; the waves of the sea were hushed. They were glad when it grew calm, and he guided them to their desired haven. Let them give thanks to

> the LORD for his unfailing love and his wonderful deeds for men. Let them exalt him in the assembly of the people and praise him in the council of the elders.
>
> —Ps. 107:28-32

Have you noticed that God is in the business of delivering people who cry out to him? His love keeps after us, pursues us, and will never let go. God loves to set his people free from fear. "For you did not receive a spirit that makes you a slave again to fear, but you received the Spirit of sonship…"

***

We cry out and God answers. What does that really mean? Does God take an active part in our lives or is he a passive observer? Does God get involved in our circumstances? What exactly does it mean that when we cry out, he answers? This next passage of the Psalm answers these questions by showing us how God works:

> He turned rivers into a desert, flowing springs into thirsty ground, and fruitful land into a salt waste, because of the wickedness of those who lived there. He turned the desert into pools of water and

> the parched ground into flowing springs; there he brought the hungry to live, and they founded a city where they could settle. They sowed fields and planted vineyards that yielded a fruitful harvest; he blessed them, and their numbers greatly increased, and he did not let their herds diminish. Then their numbers decreased, and they were humbled by oppression, calamity and sorrow; he who pours contempt on nobles made them wander in a trackless waste. But he lifted the needy out of their affliction and increased their families like flocks. The upright see and rejoice, but all the wicked shut their mouths. Whoever is wise, let him heed these things and consider the great love of the LORD.
>
> —Ps. 107:33-43

Jesus takes those things that we cling to that keep us from him and he turns them into dry, parched, and thirsty ground. Then he lifts us up and brings fruit into our lives and draws us nearer to himself. He humbles us so that we will turn to him. This becomes a process in our lives as he slowly and gently draws us into the folds of his loving arms.

God works for us as we cry out to him. The word translated "cry out" literally means "to cry in the direction of." The meaning is significant because it tells me that no motion is required. It turns out that God is more interested in direction than he is in movement. When you face in the direction of your problems and cry out...he can't hear you. When you face things with your human reasoning...he can't hear you. When you face your enemy in your own strength...God can't hear you. But when you cry out "in the direction of the Lord"...God hears and saves! Don't just dwell on your problems, bring them to Jesus and lay them at his feet.

Consider the following discourse between a Canaanite woman and Jesus:

> A Canaanite woman from that vicinity came to him, crying out, "Lord, Son of David, have mercy on me! My daughter is suffering terribly from demon possession." Jesus did not answer a word. So his disciples came to him and urged him, "Send her away, for she keeps crying out after us." He answered, "I was sent only to the lost sheep of Israel." The woman came and knelt before him.

> "Lord, help me!" she said. He replied, "It is not right to take the children's bread and toss it to their dogs." "Yes, Lord," she said, "but even the dogs eat the crumbs that fall from their masters' table." Then Jesus answered, "Woman, you have great faith! Your request is granted." And her daughter was healed from that very hour.
>
> —Matt. 15:22-28

This woman cried out to Jesus. He eventually helped her because she had no plan "B." He was her only hope.

"Crying out" is worship:

> Arise, cry out in the night, as the watches of the night begin; pour out your heart like water in the presence of the Lord. Lift up your hands to him for the lives of your children, who faint from hunger at the head of every street.
>
> —Lam. 2:19

"Crying out" is an act of desperation:

> And at the ninth hour Jesus cried out in a loud voice, "Eloi, Eloi, lama sabachthani?"— which means, "My God, my God, why have you forsaken me?"
>
> -Mark 15:34

"Crying out" is an act of poverty:

> The LORD is close to the brokenhearted and saves those who are crushed in spirit.
>
> —Ps. 34:18

"Crying out" is an act of faith:

> A man in the crowd called out, "Teacher, I beg you to look at my son, for he is my only child.
>
> —Luke 9:38

When you cry out to the Lord he will be with you because he loves you. You may not always have people around you who affirm you, but God is always present, to cherish and claim you as his son or daughter. Rejoice today in the knowledge that you are highly prized by the creator of the universe.

Life Lesson

Learning To Live Loved

Consider and discuss: Can you accept this verse:

> Give thanks to the LORD, for he is good; his love endures forever.
>
> —Ps. 107:1

Can you accept the fact that no matter what you have done God's love for you never ceases? How does this truth make you feel?

Which of the testimonies of this Psalm do you personally relate to? Why? Has there been a time when you cried out to Jesus? How did he save you from your distress?

How does it make you feel knowing that you are highly prized by the creator of the universe?

Psalm 139

Hope for the Poor in Spirit

"Blessed are the poor in spirit, for theirs is the kingdom of heaven."

—Matt. 5:3

I am convinced that one of the major problems today is that many people simply don't know who they are. I think we are in the midst of a global identity crisis. The prevailing secular world view teaches us that our earth is a tiny speck in a vast universe, and that we are struggling mortals on an obscure planet located in a second rate galaxy among billions of other galaxies.

Christians especially suffer from an identity crisis because we don't know who we are "in Christ." As Christians, we may consider what Christ means to us, but few ever consider what we mean to Christ. Let me suggest to you that you are on this planet for a reason and that your purpose is to glorify God and enjoy him forever; and that God's purpose is to glorify you and enjoy you forever. It's actually pretty simple.

The Bible is filled with men and women who suffered from an identity crisis. Some of the greats didn't know who they were. Take Moses for example. When God commanded Moses to go, he responded with, "Who am I that I should go to Pharaoh" (Ex. 3:11). Young David also responded with, "who am I," when offered King Saul's daughter. In spite of being a giant slayer, and champion of Israel, he didn't know who he was.

***

Psalm 139

Psalm 139 describes a man who is thinking about who he is and his relationship with God.

> O LORD, you have searched me and you know me.
>
> —Ps. 139:1

God knows you. He knows everything about you? How does it make you feel knowing that he sees it all? You can't hide who you are from God. "If we had forgotten the name of our God or spread out our hands to a foreign god, would not God have discovered it, since he knows the secrets of the heart?" (Ps. 44:20-21).

God knows us completely and yet there is a sense from Psalm 139 that He is still searching. Maybe he searches us the way a sculptor scrutinizes his masterpiece. Even though he created it and knows it intimately, he still runs his hand over it to cherish and enjoy every line and curve. Consider the relationship between us and our creator as David described it to his son Solomon:

> And you, my son Solomon, acknowledge the God of your father, and serve him with wholehearted devotion and with a willing mind, for the LORD searches every heart and understands every motive behind the thoughts. If you seek him, he will be found by you; but if you forsake him, he will reject you forever.
>
> —1 Chr. 28:9

God searches — we seek. It's about connecting in an eternal relationship.

God is pursuing you today. Just as he called out for Adam in the garden, he is calling out for you today. Why does God want to know us so intimately? Knowledge and love are intimately linked. The more I know about God, the more I love him, and the more I love him, the more I desire to know. This must be the way it is with God. He loves us totally because He knows us totally.

There is an old song with lyrics that say: "To know, know, know you, is to love, love, love you." I think that song gets it right.

Knowledge is the key to love. The more I know you, the real you, the more I love you. The more I intimately know God, the more I love him. The more we all know each other, and understand each other, the more we become the church, one body, under Christ, united in love.

> My purpose is that they may be encouraged in heart and united in love, so that they may have the full riches of complete understanding, in order that they may know the mystery of God, namely, Christ.
>
> —Col. 2:2

Do you love yourself? Do you love God's creation in you, believing that you are fearfully and wonderfully made? If not, then the problem is that you don't know yourself. If you could see yourself through God's eyes, if you could see the picture of the wonderful, beautiful creation you are, unique and perfect in his eyes, then you would love yourself just the way you are.

It's possible to read this Psalm and understand it in a negative way, that God searches us and finds the sin, that He knows everything and that we're in big trouble. Do you ever feel that way? The book of Job tells us the truth of how God feels about our sin:

> You will call and I will answer you; you will long for the creature your hands have made. Surely then you will count my steps but not keep track of my sin. My offenses will be sealed up in a bag; you will cover over my sin.
>
> —Job 14:15-17

This is the picture of grace. God counts every one of our steps, but he forgets our sin. He already knows every intimate detail but finds great joy in rediscovering.

> You know when I sit and when I rise; you perceive my thoughts from afar. You discern my going out and my lying down; you are familiar with all my ways. Before a word is on my tongue you know it completely, O LORD.
>
> —Ps. 139:2-4

God knows when we are passive and when we are active. He knows our conscious and subconscious thoughts. He knows everything about us, all the choices we make, all our habits. God knows everything there is to know. There is no chance that he could ever misunderstand you.

> You hem me in — behind and before; you have laid your hand upon me.
>
> —Ps. 139:5

"You hem me in — behind and before." This can sound confining and constricting and have a bad connotation, but not when you are hemmed in by the love of a God who died for you. "Behind and before..." The huge love that God has for you causes him to pursue you from behind — from your past. He goes back into your past and repairs the damage that you have caused with your unbelief. Then He enters your future and prepares a place for you that he planned before you were born. He is also in your present and has "laid his hand on [you]." And when God lays his hand on you it's not like when your dad laid his hand on you when he caught you sneaking out after curfew, but the way a loving father gently puts his affirming hand on the shoulder of his beloved son or daughter.

God is not a passive observer. He is involved in our lives. He loved us in our past, he is here now in our present with his hand on us, and the future belongs to him as he waits to bless us.

> Such knowledge is too wonderful for me, too lofty for me to attain.
>
> —Ps. 139:6

That's an understatement. I am overwhelmed that God loves me this much. God has his hand on us and apparently he's not letting go:

> Where can I go from your Spirit? Where can I flee from your presence? If I go up to the heavens, you are there; if I make my bed in the depths, you are there. If I rise on the wings of the dawn, if I settle on the far side of the sea, even there your

> hand will guide me; your right hand will hold me fast.
>
> —Ps. 139:7-10

No circumstance can separate you from God's presence. God owns and runs his universe, he is everywhere present in it and he is holding on to you. There is nowhere you could go, no situation you could be in, where God is not there to guide you and hold you. "'Am I only a God nearby,' declares the LORD, 'and not a God far away? Can anyone hide in secret places so that I cannot see him?' declares the LORD. 'Do not I fill heaven and earth?' declares the LORD'" (Jer. 23:23-24).

> If I say, "Surely the darkness will hide me and the light become night around me," even the darkness will not be dark to you; the night will shine like the day, for darkness is as light to you. Not even darkness keeps me from your vigilant eye.
>
> —Ps. 139:11-12

We are different than God. For us, some things are light and some darkness. We experience happiness, prosperity, and success and think of it as light. We experience emotional and mental pain, disappointment, losses, broken relationships, confusion, and sickness and call it darkness. But everything is light to God. He sees everything as it is and he knows the end of it; "we know that in all things God works for the good of those who love him, who have been called according to his purpose" (Rom 8:28). God takes those things we see as light and those things we see as darkness and he uses them all to bring us into the light of his presence.

> For you created my inmost being; you knit me together in my mother's womb. I praise you because I am fearfully and wonderfully made; your works are wonderful, I know that full well.
>
> —Ps. 139:13-14

Don't miss the significance of this passage. God created your inmost being, which includes your personality. To be knit together in your mother's womb means that you were handmade, very special. Inside and out you are a product of the master craftsman's handiwork. He hopes that you like his work. He hopes that you respond as David did: "I praise you because I am fearfully and wonderfully made; your works are wonderful." Sometimes I think that I have been made more fearfully than most. But the word "fearfully" means "awesome." The author is marveling in the awesome creativity of God.

Actually to be fearfully and wonderfully made means that we are made in God's image. He made us so we would look like him. What! How can that be? Imagine the greatest football player of all time? Suppose he had a son? Would there be a good chance that the son would be an athlete? Suppose his son never played sports, never exercised, spent his youth sitting in front of the TV. Would he be a great athlete? Would you say his dad didn't give him the ability or that he had the ability but never took hold of it? So, God created you in his own image. Do you think you look like God? To be created in God's image is to have his characteristics…to be like him. This is the work God wants to finish in each of our lives. We are fearfully and wonderfully made. He wants to finish what he started and take hold of our destiny.

> My frame was not hidden from you when I was made in the secret place, when I

> was woven together in the depths of the earth.
>
> —Ps. 139:15

You have been carefully created like fine intricate embroidery. God is very creative and when he made you he got real fancy. You are the deluxe version.

> Your eyes saw my unformed body. All the days ordained for me were written in your book before one of them came to be.
>
> —Ps. 139:16

You are not a static creation. God didn't just make you for show. He has a dream and a purpose for you. Before you were born he ordained your days. Are you living the days that he ordained for you? Are you living the victory, joy, wholeness and fulfillment that he planned? The verse said he saw your unformed body. Maybe he's not done creating you yet.

Now the Psalm takes a sudden and disturbing turn. The psalmist is saying, "God, since you know me so well, since you are so close, since you made me the way I am, I am going to be honest with you. I'm going to open up and tell you how I really feel:

> If only you would slay the wicked, O God! Away from me, you bloodthirsty men! They speak of you with evil intent; your adversaries misuse your name. Do I not hate those who hate you, O LORD, and abhor those who rise up against you? I have nothing but hatred for them; I count them my enemies.
>
> —Ps. 139:19-22

"Lord — kill the wicked!" Where did that come from? What happened to "Love your enemies; pray for those who despitefully use you?" Right or wrong, he is being honest with God about his feelings. He asks God to enter into and judge those feelings:

> Search me, O God, and know my heart; test me and know my anxious thoughts. See if there is any offensive way in me, and lead me in the way everlasting.
>
> —Ps. 139:23-24

What a great prayer. Lord you know me better than I know myself and you care for me more than I care for myself. David is saying, "Search me Lord, test me, put me on trial, judge me, and separate the truth in my life from the error. Know my anxious thoughts. Know those thoughts that rob me of my peace. Lord, see if there is any wickedness in me — anything that I put before you that will hurt you, or will hurt me because it will deprive me of fellowship with you. Lord, keep me from wickedness, the way of pain."

"Lead me in the way everlasting." Everlasting life has already begun; we are in it now. Death isn't meant to be an interruption of our life, but merely a transition from time to timeless. For the sinner, death is like a raging river; when crossing you are swept away. But to the Christian, death is just a little creek to hop over and continue your journey. David is asking God to lead him in the way that will put him on the right path. The idea isn't that God will discover how really wicked we are and then pounce on us. David wants to have a heart like God. He wants to get everything out of his life that isn't supposed to be there.

God doesn't come to us as the hanging judge. His judgment for Christians is meant to be a dividing, a separating. He wants to separate us from those things that keep us from enjoying fellowship with him. He wants to separate us from those things that keep him from putting us up on display for all eternity as his workmanship, his masterpiece, and the very best of all his creation.

The secret to being rich in spirit is to begin to see yourself the way God views you. Ask him to show you today.

Life Lesson

Knowing who we are in Christ

Consider and discuss: Do you ever feel out of place or that you don't belong?

Do you believe that God made you and that you are on this planet for a purpose? Can you articulate God's purpose for you?

Psalm 139:1 says:

> O LORD, you have searched me and you know me.

How does it make you feel knowing that God knows everything about you? Elaborate.

This Psalm tells us that God was active in our past, our future, and that his hand is on us today. Describe what it means to have God active and involved in your life.

God says we are fearfully and wonderfully made. How does that line up with how you see yourself? Explain.

Pray and ask God to give you the picture of yourself as he sees you.

About the Author

Bob Saffrin lives in Minneapolis, Minnesota with Barb, his wife of 46 years, and their beagle Rocky. Bob and Barb have two children and four grandchildren. Bob loves the outdoors and has been on many backpacking trips in the rugged Boundary Waters Area of Minnesota, including winter camping. In his 20s, Bob began a fascination with the Bible. After reading the New Testament several times and convinced that Jesus had died on the cross to save him, Bob asked Jesus into his life and began a wonderful lifelong relationship. His fascination with the Bible became a love for God and for his word. Bob has been teaching and preaching for over 35 years.

Contact Bob Saffrin at: www.bobsaffrin.com

Other books by Bob Saffrin:

Moses, Steps to a Life of Faith

Elijah, Steps to a Life of Power

Psalm 23, Help for Lost Lambs

How to Sleep Like a Baby, a Meditation on Psalm 3

Appendix

Bible exercise for relieving stress so you can sleep — from Psalm 3:

Read the Psalm 3 chapter first.

David started out his prayer with simply acknowledging who God is: *But you are a shield around me, O Lord" (Psalm 3:3a).*

Step 1: Read and meditate on the following verses that all speak to **who God is:**

Oh, God how majestic is your Name above all the earth (Psalm 8:1).

Know that the Lord is God. It is he who made us (Psalm 100:3).

As for God, his way is perfect; the word of the Lord is flawless. He is a shield for all who take refuge in him (2 Samuel 22:31).

The Lord is my shepherd, I shall not be in want (Psalm 23:1).

God is love — The Lord is gracious and compassionate, slow to anger and rich in love (Psalm 145:8).

The Eternal God, your Refuge (Deut 33:27a).

...the Sun of Righteousness (Malachi 4:2b).

God is Faithful (1 Cor. 10:13b).

Captain of the Host of the Lord (Josh. 5:14).

The Lord is your keeper; The Lord is your shade on your right hand (Psalm 121:5).

I am the Lord who exercises kindness, justice and righteousness on the earth (Jer. 9:24).

Exalt the LORD our God and worship at his holy mountain, for the LORD our God is holy (Psalm 99:9).

God is our refuge and strength, an ever-present help in trouble (Psalm 46:1).

After reading the above verses read through them one more time; focus and meditate on who God is. (Selah)

Next David focused on what God does: *you lift my head.*

Step 2: Read the following verses that tell us **what God does:**

...to comfort all who mourn, and provide for those who grieve in Zion — to bestow on them a crown of beauty instead of ashes, the oil of gladness instead of mourning, and a garment of praise instead of a spirit of despair (Isaiah 61:2-3).

Rather, worship the Lord your God; it is he who will deliver you from the hand of all your enemies (2 Kings 17:39).

It is God who arms me with strength and makes my way perfect (Psalms 18:32).

You have filled my heart with greater joy than when their grain and new wine abound (Psalms 4:7).

The Lord is faithful to all his promises and loving toward all he has made (Psalms 145:13).

He holds us in his everlasting arms (Deut 33:27).

...will arise with healing in his wings (Malachi 4:2).

...He will not let you be tempted beyond what you can bear... (1Cor. 10:13).

He brought me out of the pit of destruction, out of the miry clay; and He set my feet upon a rock making my footsteps firm (Psalm 40:2).

The Lord will protect you from all evil; He will keep your soul. The Lord will guard your going out and your coming in from this time forth and forever (Psalm 121:7-8).

The LORD is close to the brokenhearted and saves those who are crushed in spirit (Psalm 34:18).

The LORD Almighty is with us; the God of Jacob is our fortress (Psalm 46:7).

LORD, there is no one like you to help the powerless against the mighty (2 Chronicles 14:11).

For he has not despised or disdained the suffering of the afflicted one; he has not hidden his face from him but has listened to his cry for help (Psalm 22:24).

O LORD my God, I called to you for help and you healed me. O LORD, you brought me up from the grave; you spared me from going down into the pit (Ps 30:2-3).

I will lie down and sleep in peace, for you alone, O LORD, make me dwell in safety (Psalm 4:8).

After reading the above verses, read through them again and meditate on what God does. (Selah)

Next, David thought about how God has always been there for him when he cried out to him: *I cry out and you answer me.*

Step 3: Read the following verses on how **God is there for us when we cry out to him**.

I sought the Lord, and he answered me; he delivered me from all my fears (Psalms 34:4).

The Lord is near to all who call on him, to all who call on him in truth. He fulfills the desires of those who fear him; he hears their cry and saves them (Psalms 145:18-19).

The eternal God is your refuge, and underneath are the everlasting arms. He will drive out your enemy before you, saying, "Destroy him!" (Deuteronomy 33:27).

But for you who revere my name, the sun of righteousness will rise with healing in its wings (Malachi 4:2).

No temptation has seized you except what is common to man. And God is faithful; he will not let you be tempted beyond what you can bear. But when you are tempted, he will also provide a way out so that you can stand up under it (1 Corinthians 10:13).

...call upon me in the day of trouble; I will deliver you, and you will honor me" (Psalms 50:15).

My help comes from the Lord, the Maker of heaven and earth. He will not let your foot slip — he who watches over you will not slumber; (Psalms 121:2-3).

...I am in deep distress. Let us fall into the hands of the LORD, for his mercy is great! (2 Sam 24:14).

...What other nation is so great as to have their gods near them the way the LORD our God is near us whenever we pray to him? (Deut 4:7).

For this is what the high and lofty One says — he who lives forever, whose name is holy: "I live in a high and holy place, but also with him who is contrite and lowly in spirit" (Isaiah 57:15).

Blessed are the poor in spirit, for theirs is the kingdom of heaven (Isa 57:15).

With your help I can advance against a troop; with my God I can scale a wall (Ps 18:29).

The LORD gives strength to his people; the LORD blesses his people with peace (Ps. 29:11).

If you still do not have peace…start over with step 1.

Sleep well!

Made in the USA
San Bernardino, CA
24 January 2013